THE
ONE
THING
NEEDFUL

WILLIAM MASON

The One Thing Needful

The Believer's Pocket Companion

William Mason

CCR PUBLICATIONS

CHRIST CHURCH – RADFORD

ORIGINAL TITLE:

THE BELIEVER'S POCKET COMPANION

THE ONE THING NEEDFUL TO MAKE POOR SINNERS RICH
—AND MISERABLE SINNERS HAPPY

This edition Copyright © 2015 by Christ Church — Radford
Author: William Mason (1719 – 1791)

Published by CCR Publications
        a publishing ministry of Christ Church — Radford
        6226 University Park Drive
        Radford, VA 24141
        christchurchradford.org

All Rights Reserved. No part of this book may be copied or reproduced without written permission from the publisher.

This edition is a revision of the original edition published in 1773 entitled:

        The Believer's Pocket Companion
        The One Thing Needful to Make Poor Sinners Rich
        —and Miserable Sinners Happy

All rights reserved. No part of this publication may be reproduced, stored in a retrieval system, or transmitted in any form by any means, electronic, mechanical, photocopy, recording, or otherwise, without the prior permission of the publisher, except as provided by USA copyright law.

Cover design and Interior design: Jon Green

Printed in the United States of America

Please visit our website at:
christchurchradford.org

ISBN: 978-1-5147-7415-1

Table of Contents

Preface 9

Putting on Christ,
    The One Thing Needful 11

Who Are Exhorted
    To Put On Christ 15

What Is Implied
    In Putting On Christ 23

How to Put On Christ
    In Our Minds 31

How to Put On Christ
    In Our Memory 39

How to Put On Christ
    In Our Conscience 43

Why We Should
    Put On Christ 51

When We Should
    Put On Christ 75

Happy Consequences
    of Thus Putting On Christ 99

On the Use and Abuse
    of Past Experience 113

Other Books
from C.C.R. Publishing:
    131

Preface

"Christ is all!" – *Colossians 3:2*

*"Put on the Lord Jesus Christ,
and make not provision for the flesh,
to fulfill the lusts thereof."*

– *Romans 13:14*

What do you think of Christ? This is the most important question in the world. Happy for that sinner who can answer it from his heart and say, "Christ is precious to me!"

For such this little work is intended. To such it is humbly addressed. The design of it being to stir up and quicken such in the way of believing in Christ, looking to Christ, coming unto him, and abiding in him; or, in the apostle's words, "to be putting on the Lord Jesus Christ"—so that they may enjoy more sweet fellowship with him, find more of the inestimable preciousness of him, and experience more of his wonderful love, which passes knowledge.

I do, and hope I shall to my latest breath, insist upon it, that all is not right between Christ and the soul, if it is not earnestly desiring to maintain constant, uninterrupted, holy fellowship with him, studiously pursuing those means which tend to promote the life and power of practical, experimental godliness, and avoiding all things which are contrary to our most holy faith.

With a humble desire, and sincere aim to excite to this, the following work is intended. Dear reader, it is contrived for your pocket, and intended for your heart. I beseech you to accept it in love—to overlook the faults you find in it—and to look up for a blessing upon it, and the author of it.

W. M.

August 9, 1773

Chapter 1

Putting on Christ,
The One Thing Needful

The following observations, upon the present state of religion in this land, are very obvious:

1. There never was a time in which the precious truths of the gospel, and the glorious doctrines of grace, were treated with so much calumny, contempt and ridicule, by the professors of Christianity, as in the present day[1]. This is a most dreadful consideration. For this, we may justly dread the most sore and impending judgments to be executed upon this sinful land.

2. Yet, this is a day, in which the Lord is sending forth many laborers into his vineyard, who preach the everlasting gospel with great clearness, power and faithfulness; and which gospel the Lord causes to have free course, to run and be glorified, to the gathering in of multitudes of precious souls to Christ, to whom he gives to live and walk in the rich experience, and sweet enjoyment of his pardoning love, jus-

---
1 This was written in 1773.

tifying grace, comforting peace, and sanctifying influence. This is a most joyful reflection. This, a favorable signal to our sinful nation. But still,

3. Though, perhaps, there never was a greater profession of Christ, and of the truth as it in him, than in this day; yet many, very many professors content themselves with the form of godliness—instead of the power; the mere notion of truth—instead of the experience of it; the name of faith—instead of the grace of faith; the mere profession of Christ—instead of the actual possession of him. How few really feel their hearts happy in him, their hopes centered on him, and then affections going out after him! Hence they are not devoted in life and walk to the glory of Christ. This calls for much self-examination, and great searching of heart.

In view of it, "My heart is inditing good matter." O for the pen of a ready writer, to set forth the matchless glory and unparalleled excellence of the King—*the King of Kings*—the King of saints, even King Jesus; your King and mine! You once stout hearted rebels against his crown and government! But, O the love of his royal heart! Instead of executing fierce vengeance upon us, for our sins, lo, he came from heaven to earth, with a flame of love in his heart, and matchless grace on his lips, on purpose to die for us, to wash us from our sins in his own blood, to conquer the rebellion of our hearts against him, and to win our affections to him. Has he saved us by his precious blood? Has he made us his willing, loving disciples, by his powerful grace? Surely, it is that we should live in the sweet enjoyment of all the rich blessings of his kingdom, and be holy and happy every day, yes, every hour, *in him*. In life and love be wholly devoted to him.

But whence then those sighs and complaints—those doubts and fears—those jealousies and suspicions, which so rend the hearts of disciples, distress their spirits, and dishonor their dear Lord and Savior? Come they not hence? Though they may be espoused to Christ, yet they are not chaste virgins to him—they do not cleave to him with full purpose of heart—they do not live on him by faith—they do not obey his precious word, a*bide in me.* O you burdened disciples, hear and receive your Lord's loving reproof, "You are anxious and troubled about many things: *But one thing is needful*" (Luke 10:42). O for a single eye to look unto Jesus, a humble heart to sit at his feet, and a simple soul to hear and believe every word from his gracious lips, that we may know the love of Christ—constantly know it by a heartfelt sense of it. This, this is the one thing needful, to make poor sinners rich, and miserable sinners happy in time, and joyful to all eternity!

Know your calling, beloved of Christ. Consider your one business. Remember your chief employment. It is not merely to make a profession, and to keep up a form of godliness—but to maintain and keep up a warm, lively, comfortable sense of the love of Christ in your hearts, from day to day, yes, from hour to hour. How is this to be done? there is but one way. The Holy Spirit of Truth, the glorifier of Christ, the sanctifier and comforter of his disciples, directs us to this one way, by his servant Paul: *"put on the Lord Jesus Christ"* (Rom. 13:14).

Let us indulge a few meditations upon these precious words. "Lord, help us to see the glory that shines in them, to exercise our minds upon them, so as to put them into practice, that we may draw sweet consolation from them." Let us consider, 1—W*ho* are here exhorted.

2 — *What* is implied in the exhortation, "put on Christ".
3 — *Why* we should put on Christ. 4 — *When* we should put him on, and lastly, 5 — *the blessed effects* and happy consequences of thus putting on Christ.

> *Brethren, let us praise our Lord:*
> *Exalt his blessed name:*
> *Let us hear and keep his word*
> *His glory be our aim.*
>
> *Let us resolutely strive*
> *To work God's work with full intent.*
> *And what is it? To believe*
> *On Christ whom he has sent.*

Chapter 2

Who Are Exhorted
To Put On Christ

O marvelous mystery of astonishing grace! Sinners! You who see, know and feel yourselves to be nothing but sin—yes, the very chief of sinners—have a right, by free gift, of free grace—to take, possess, and put on Christ! The poor souls who are dead in trespasses and sins, have all got self-righteous hearts, because their understandings are blind, and their consciences are stupid. To exhort such to put on Christ, would be as foolish and as vain, as to bid a dead corpse arise, and put on clothing. But it is you—quickened, enlightened, sensible sinners, whose consciences smart for sin, whose hearts ache for the curses of the law denounced against sin, and whose spirits tremble to be found in your own righteousness; it is you—afflicted, tempest-tossed, and not comforted by anything that you can find and feel in yourselves; who see your own nakedness, and constantly view your own righteousness as filthy rags—who are exhorted to put on Christ.

Paul best knew whom he exhorted. He describes them in the beginning of this epistle thusly; "To all those that are in Rome, *beloved of God*" (Rom. 1:7). None but those loved by God the Father have any saving interest in, or have anything to do with Christ his beloved Son. But how did it appear that these sinners at Rome were, or that any sinners now, are loved by God? Truly, as plainly as though the love of God were written in legible characters upon their foreheads. This is clearly manifest by these two plain and express evidences.

1. They were called to be saints.
2. Their faith was spoken of, verse 7 and 8. That sinner who is favored with these special and peculiar graces, to be loved by God, and to have faith in and from the Son of God, may be as well assured that he is called by God, as though the voice of an archangel, or the voice of God himself, proclaimed it from heaven to his ears.

First, let us consider our calling. "Remember, dear brothers and sisters, that few of you were wise in the world's eyes, or powerful, or wealthy *when God called you*. Instead, God deliberately chose things the world considers *foolish* in order to shame those who think they are wise. And he chose those who are *powerless* to shame those who are powerful. God chose things *despised* by the world, things counted as nothing at all, and used them to bring to nothing what the world considers important, so that no one can ever boast in the presence of God" (1 Cor. 1:26-29).

O, we do not enough dwell upon the infinite love, discriminating grace, and almighty power of the Lord—in effectually calling us, poor sinners—from sin, death, and hell—to righteousness, life, and heaven, in Jesus! What! has the Lord singled you out, and separated you from a world of dead sinners, to hear his mighty voice, and to obey his loving call? Have you heard the sweet, loving, and persuasive voice of the dear Shepherd, saying, "Come unto me!" O remember, this is because you are loved by God. The effectual calling of Christ is the fruit of the everlasting love of God. Sinners being loved by God, and given to Christ in eternity, they must be effectually called—they must come to Christ in time.

As love—infinite, everlasting immutable love, is the cause from which our calling proceeds; so the end of our calling is, to put on, possess, and enjoy Christ Jesus. For we are called to be saints *in* him.

Secondly, Paul addresses those who had faith. This is a grace of new covenant love. It is a precious gift, which is bestowed upon all those loved by God. It is a grace peculiar to them only. Therefore it is called, "the faith of God's elect" (Titus 1:1). "Not all have faith" (2 Thess. 3:2). O believer, remember, there was a time when you had not one grain of the precious grace of faith. Ever consider—who is God's elect (Isa. 42:1). Ever consider—that Jesus is the *author* and *object* of your faith. So surely as your faith fixes upon Christ as its only object for life and salvation, so surely are you loved by God, and chosen by God. This you may be as sure of, as though Christ was now upon earth, and told you so with his infallible lips of truth.

Faith manifests itself to be of God, and proves that the believer is beloved of God, and born of God—

1. By receiving and setting to its seal, to the *truth* of God, respecting the sinner's own state. If you are a be-

liever, you have just the same views of yourself, as the word of God sets forth to you. You are sensible, that in yourself, you are a poor, wretched, miserable, blind, naked sinner—that you have the sentence of death in yourself—that you have neither hope nor help in and from yourself for salvation—you know and feel from day to day, that in your flesh dwells no good thing—that sin abounds in you—that your nature is totally corrupt and abominable, and your heart deceitful above all things, and desperately wicked—that when you would do good, evil is present with you—that of yourself you are not sufficient to think a good thought—that in all you aim to do to please God, you come short of his glory, and of your duty—that after you have done all, you see yourself an unprofitable servant in all—are ever dissatisfied with yourself and with all your works and doings; for you see all your own righteousness to be nothing better than filthy rags. Therefore you can have no trust in yourself— you dare place no confidence in the flesh—you have no dependence on your own works. For, faith has brought the truths of God into your heart. You have not only the notion of them in your head—but you find the inward sense and experience of them in your very soul. Thus, you are cast into the humbling mold of God's truth, by the grace of faith. While proud, self-righteous hearts, are strangers to the humbling grace of faith, and see not the constant need they have of putting on the Lord Jesus Christ—you daily see the necessity of this, and you, as a beloved child of God, are exhorted to this.

2. Faith manifests itself to be of God, as the believing sinner judges of himself according to the *law* of God. God's law is a transcript of his holy mind and will. Faith receives it, as a right rule of just judgment. You believe and confess, that the law is holy, and the commandment is holy, and just, and good; and that sin by the commandment has become exceedingly sinful in your sight. For, by the law is the knowledge of sin. Therefore you see yourself cursed by the law, a transgressor against its just, holy, and righteousness precepts. You behold the law as a ministration of condemnation. It condemns you as a sinner, for all that you are in yourself, and in all that you do, for you ever come short of its perfect demands. Your mouth is stopped. You are guilty. You have no plea in yourself, why you should not suffer its curse and wrath to all eternity. It speaks nothing but wrath to you. It works wrath in your conscience. Though you love the holy law, and delight in it after the inward man, yet you find that the law has become weak through the flesh, and therefore you see that you are no more able to fulfill the righteousness of the law, than you are to avert its wrath and curses. Both are as impossible to you, as to create a world. Therefore you see and confess, that by the deeds of the law no flesh living can be justified in God's sight; for by the law is the knowledge of sin (Rom. 3:20).

*"For to convince, and to condemn,
is all the law can do."*

Still you honor the law of God, by believing its purity and perfection. You honor the *wisdom* of God in giving the law, that the offense might abound. You honor the *justice* of God, by believing his judgment is just, in pronouncing you cursed, because you have not continued in all things which are written in the law to do them. You honor the *truth* of God by believing—that unless every righteous precept of the law is perfectly fulfilled, all its curses suffered, and all its penalties inflicted—you, a guilty sinner, could never be saved. Hence you see the necessity of putting on Christ, and being clothed with his righteousness, who is the end of the law for righteousness to everyone who believes (Rom. 10:4).

3. Faith manifests itself to be of God, by gladly receiving the *gospel* of his grace — the ministration of righteousness — the glad tidings of free, full, and finished salvation, by the life and death of his dear son. The God of truth and you are agreed. He puts all his honor and glory upon the Son of his love. You acquiesce herein. The Father loves the Son; so do you. The Father says, "This is my beloved Son. Believe him. Hear him." You answer, "I love his voice — I delight to hear and obey the precious words of life and salvation from my Savior's lips. To whom should I go? Whom should I hear, but you, O Son of God? For you only, have the words of eternal life, to speak to me, a lost sinner."

The Father has committed all your salvation to the Son. Faith leads you to rejoice in this. You honor the Son, even as you honor the Father. You honor the Father, by receiving the record which he has given of eternal life in his Son. You honor the Son in believing on him for eternal life. You honor his precious blood, by believing it to be the one atonement for sin, and that there is a redemption and forgiveness of sins in his blood alone. You honor his life of obedience, by believing that thereby the holy law is perfectly fulfilled, and an everlasting righteousness wrought out; which being imputed to you a sinner, you stand completely justified in the sight of God. And where the faith of Christ is thus in the heart, it works by the love of Christ, and love to Christ; and that soul is disposed to cleave to Christ, loves to enjoy communion with Christ; and in life, delights to be wholly devoted to the glory of Christ.

4. Faith gives evidence that it comes from God, as the believing soul loves holiness, and hates iniquity. Sin, which he once "dead in", he is now "dead to". Son, which was once his chief delight, is now his greatest burden. He groans under the body of sin, which he carries about with him, yet it has always a dwelling in him. Therefore he abhors himself, and detests sin from his heart. He know that sin separates between a holy God, and a sinful creature. He views the evil of sin, and the curses due to it, in the cross and sufferings of his Savior. He believes that the blood of God was shed to expiate sin; and that so deep was its dye, that nothing less could atone for its malignancy, and take away its guilt. He believes sin to be the abominable thing which God's soul hates. He dreads committing sin, for fear of contracting guilt. He fears, lest he should grieve the Spirit, lose his comforts, and cause his Father to frown upon him, which would bring a hell of distress, instead of heaven of love into his conscience. Faith takes its view of sin from the divine word, and the wrath of God therein revealed against it. The believer strives against sin, as being contrary to the holy nature of his heavenly Father, and inconsistent with his state, as a son God, and a new creature in Jesus Christ. Hence, he cannot continue in sin, because grace abounds. Seeing the abounding of God's grace to him, keeps up the fight against sin within him. Faith keeps up his hope, of being perfectly delivered from the being of sin; and keeps him constantly warring against the sin which is in his members. By Faith he looks and cries to Jesus, to save him from sin, as well as from wrath. Such is the nature if the precious faith of God's elect. Well then is the faith of the gospel called a *most holy faith* (Jude 20).

Dear reader, examine, have you received this precious faith? If you have, though it be but as a gain of mustard seed, ever so small, and ever so weak, yet, you, even you, are beloved of God the Father—you are the called of his beloved Son, you are a saint in Christ; you, even you, vile as you may be in your own eyes, condemned as you may be in your own sight—yet you are the very quickened soul, the very sensible sinner, the very living believer, who is here addressed by Paul, and exhorted, *Put on the lord Jesus Christ.*

> *Lamb of God, we fall before thee,*
>   *Humbly trusting in your cross:*
> *That alone be all our glory;*
>   *All things else are dung and dross.*
> *You we own a perfect Savior,*
>   *Only source of all that's good.*
> *Every grace, and every favor*
>   *Comes to us thro' Jesus' blood.*

Is it so? — then, as a poor sinner, put on this perfect Savior—ever glory in His perfection—and rejoice that you are *perfect in Him.*

Chapter 3

What Is Implied
In Putting On Christ

A Believer in Christ exhorted to put on Christ! Why, Paul positively asserts, "As many as have been baptized into Christ, have put on Christ" (Gal. 3:27). As all believers are baptized into Christ by one Spirit and have all put on Christ; how is it then, that they are here exhorted again to put on Christ? True, that very moment a sinner believes on Christ, he puts on Christ as his atonement, righteousness and salvation. He is united to, and is one with Christ. His sins are pardoned in the blood of Christ; his soul is justified in the righteousness of Christ, and he has everlasting life in Christ. This, this is the most precious truth. This is the glory of faith. This is the joy and rejoicing of the believing soul.

But then, before such a soul arrives to the full enjoyment of Christ in eternal glory, he has many enemies to encounter—many trials and troubles to conflict with—a body of sin and death to be delivered from—many lusts to be mortified—many corruptions to be subdued—a legion of sins to strive against—holiness to be perfected—graces to be exercised—duties to be performed—in one word, he has to glorify Christ in the world, by his life and walk. How is all this to be done? Only by Christ strengthening him. Therefore he is constantly to put on Christ—to attain a greater knowledge of Christ—more rich and sweet experience of his grace and love—to be more strongly rooted in his love, and confirmed in his salvation—to have his heart, his hopes, his affections more with Christ—and his soul more swallowed up in the ocean of God's everlasting love in Christ, that he may be more conformed to the image of Christ.

Thus, as a good soldier of Christ, he may manfully fight under his banner against the world, the flesh, and the devil, unto his life's end. That you may do this, cheerfully and comfortably, you are exhorted to put on Christ, which clearly holds forth to us,

1. The believer's interest in Christ, and the free and constant use which he is called upon to make of Christ. O consider, Christ is given to us, to be enjoyed by us. He gave himself for us, that we might receive, possess, and put him on, for all the blessed purposes of his life and death, his love, grace and salvation. He is the *bread of life*. We are to feed upon him daily. He is the *water of life*, which our souls are to drink of constantly. He is our *righteousness*. We are to put him on continually. So that we not only *have* precious Christ—but we are also to *use* him—and enjoy his preciousness. He is not only a well of salvation—but we must draw water out of it with joy, and drink of it to the refreshing of our souls!

It was not enough that the brazen serpent was set up—but it was to be looked unto, that those who were stung might be cured. It is not enough that we have faith by which to live—but we must live by the faith we have upon the Son of God, so as to derive a continual supply of grace, comfort, and strength from him, as the branch does sap from the root, the members influence from the head, and the pipe waters from the fountain.

> *"I live by faith in the Son of God, who loved me and gave himself for me!"* – *Galatians 2:20.*

The believer has a perfect sanctification, as well as a perfect justification, in his Lord and Saviour. In his approaches to a throne of grace, he looks beyond both guilt and graces in himself, pleading the salvation of Jesus only. Christ crucified is the source of peace, acceptance, and humble boldness; also of inward fruits and heart holiness. Sin cannot be mortified, but by looking to him who hung upon the cross for its atonement; and beholding the glory of God in the face, person, and undertaking of Jesus, is the only thing that transforms the soul into the same image. — Christ is the tree of life, both root and branch; the temple, the altar, and the sacrifice; the giver and the gift; the all in all of a believer's dependence. Christ, thus apprehended, is the cause of holiness, in the bud, blossom, and fruit. Christ is a cordial in times of fainting; a door of hope in times of trouble and temptation; a healer of spiritual sickness; a setter of bones, when broken by willful sin or aggravated backsliding; an altar, sanctifying every gift that is offered upon it; a fountain, watering his own graces in the heart: the spring of all happiness and peace, purity and holiness, here and for ever more. Our sanctification in Christ is thus complete. Holiness in his child, evidences the legitimacy of its birth; admits of different degrees; is of a growing nature here below, and will be capable of increase, perhaps in the regions of glory, where we shall meet, and be happy for ever.

Now faith is given to us, for this very purpose, to claim Christ, to use him, to put him on, to cleave to him, to glory of and in him. Hence the Holy Spirit, in order to stir up and quicken our drowsy souls, calls upon us, "Awake, awake, put on your strength, O Zion; put on your beautiful garments, O Jerusalem" (Isa. 52:1). O soul, who is your strength but Christ? What are your beautiful garments—but the rich robe of his all-perfect and ever glorious righteousness? O awake then in this glorious gospel-day! This is a blessed time of rejoicing, cast off all sloth and drowsiness! Lay aside your sorrow and mourning! Put on your Christ, and rejoice and be glad in him! Put Him on as your **Lord** to reign in and rule over you! Put Him on as your **Jesus** to save you from all your enemies! Put Him on as your **Christ**, anointed of God, to bless you with grace, and to crown you with glory.

2. Putting on Christ implies the renewed acts, and fresh applications of the believing soul to Christ, in the exercise of faith in him, hope towards him, delight in him, calling upon him, hearing the gospel of his grace preached, reading the Scriptures which testify of him, feeding upon his blessed body, and drinking his precious blood at his table, etc. In the use of all these means, we should aim to put on Christ afresh, as the glory of our hearts, and the joy of our souls. Christians are not only partakers of faith in Christ—but it's exercise is described, by their continued acts of believing in Christ, hearing of Christ, coming to him, leaning on him, cleaving to him, abiding in him, living upon him, and putting him on from day to day.

They are not satisfied with looking back, and thinking they once had faith—that they formerly had experience, and therefore may now rest in spiritual sloth, and swim down the stream of life in carnal security, just as the rest of the world do. No, no! Living faith upon a living Saviour, has a very different influence upon living souls. They cannot be contented, without putting on Christ afresh, and constantly enjoying him. This is the glory of faith.

3. To put on Christ, may more precisely mean, that we daily, yea constantly clothe our mind, memory, and conscience with Christ, and with the truth as it is in him—which truth holds forth, what he hath done for us, what he is to us, and what he is now doing for us at the right hand of God. O believer, this is most precious work, to put on Christ, for the comfort of your mind, the refreshing of your memory, and for the peace and joy of your conscience. This should be your constant, daily exercise—under a full conviction that without this inward enjoyment of Christ, you can neither be happy in your soul, comfortable in your walk, nor holy in your life. But if Christ dwells constantly in your mind, memory and conscience, all will be peaceful and happy within, all will be holiness unto him without.

But, it may be asked, what is meant by the mind, memory and conscience?

The *mind* of a Christian may imply, that renewed understanding or judgment, which God hath given him of revealed truths, by the Spirit of wisdom and revelation, in the knowledge of Christ: "the eyes of his understanding being enlightened, to know what is the hope of his calling in Christ" (Eph. 1:17,18). Hence, from minding only carnal things, he becomes 'spiritually minded'—he minds spiritual things—his mind is set on Christ, approving of the scripture truths which are centred in him, and the way of salvation by him. Thus his mind is formed for, and disposed to attend to them, to dwell on them, to delight in, and to be clothed with them. Paul says, "With the *mind* I myself serve the law of God" (Rom. 7:25). For the Lord writes his law in his people's *minds*, as he promises (Heb. 10:16). Hence it is said, "God has given us the spirit of a sound *mind*" (2 Tim. 1:7). — So that no one has a sound mind in the principles and doctrines of the gospel naturally; but it is the gift of God's grace, according to covenant love. And this sound mind, which is caused by an enlightened understanding and judgment in spiritual things, manifests itself in being exercised upon the sound, sacred, salutary truths of the gospel of God's grace, and salvation by the Son of his love — or, in the apostle's words, by putting on the Lord Jesus Christ. This is the most noble and exalted act of the mind. Hence, Christian, see wherein the blessedness of our *mind* consists.

By the Christian's *memory*, we understand that faculty of the new-born soul, which retains, recalls, and recognizes scripture truths, in their reality, power and importance. The memory is the sacred repository of them; and is like an handmaid to the mind. Therefore, Paul says, "Moreover, brethren, I declare unto you the gospel, which I preached unto you, which also you have received, and wherein ye stand; by which also ye are saved, if ye keep in *memory* what I preached unto you; unless ye have believed in vain" (1 Cor. 15:1,2). You see, what stress he lays upon the necessity of holding fast and retaining the important truths of the gospel in the memory, to the quickening of our faith, establishing our hope, animating our souls, and saving us, day by day, from sin. "Therefore, we ought to give the more earnest heed to the things which we have heard, lest, at any time, we should let them *slip:*" or, as the word signifies, *run out of* *our memory*, as liquor does out of a leaky vessel (Heb. 2:1). Hence see, the use of the memory, and the necessity of its being constantly exercised in recalling, recollecting, and retaining the things we have heard of the gospel of God's grace, and of the salvation of his Son, that we may have a lively sense of them upon our hearts. Thus be ever putting on Christ in your *memory*.

The *conscience* of the Christian is, that inward knowledge and testimony, which the soul has of its own sin and misery, by the conviction of the word and Spirit of God. Hence conscience, like an echo within, answers to the sound of the word without. The word proclaims, "All the world is become guilty before God" (Rom. 3:19). Conscience testifies, 'I feel the guilt, and dread the wrath due to it.' The Spirit testifies in the word, of pardon of sin, peace with God, and justification before God, by the blood and righteousness of the Son of God. The Christian's conscience bears the same witness within. Hence the believer hath "a good conscience" (1 Tim. 1:5). For, his heart is sprinkled by the blood of Christ, from an evil or guilty conscience (Heb. 10:22). He has also the answer of a good conscience towards God, by the resurrection of Jesus Christ from the dead (1 Pet. 3:21).—For Christ died for his sins, and rose again for his justification. This is his only plea before God, for pardon and justification. And the most delightful plea it is to God. For, hereby his law is magnified and made honorable; every attribute and perfection of Jehovah is glorified: while the poor sinner is justified, his conscience satisfied, made peaceful and happy. If then the conscience is freed from guilt; if it is made good; and obtains peace by the sprinkling of the blood of Christ; if it is furnished with a good answer to God, and to his law, by the resurrection of Christ—we see the imperative necessity of putting on the

Lord Jesus Christ in the conscience. So will it be kept undefiled by his grace; and in simplicity, and godly sincerity, we shall have our conversation in the world. The mind, memory, and conscience, being thus sweetly engaged, the affections will be inflamed with the love of Christ; and while under the warm influence of his love, our life will be cheerfully devoted to his service and glory. Let us, therefore, deeply consider these points. I shall enlarge upon them hereafter.

May the Spirit of all truth, holiness and comfort, bless our meditations, to the glory of Christ, and to the joy of our souls.

> *Happy souls, who put on Christ*
> *By pure and living faith,*
> *Finding him their King and Priest,*
> *Their God, and guide to death.*

> *God's own foe may plague his sons:*
> *Sin may distress— but can't subdue.*
> *Christ who conquered for us once,*
> *Will in us conquer too.*

Chapter 4

How to Put On Christ
In Our Minds

People say, "My mind is *my* kingdom." Poor souls! What do they mean? This—to have their own wills to reign, and the desires of their flesh and their minds gratified. Ah—but it is a sad kingdom, where Christ does not reign in the mind. Yes, it is a kingdom of darkness, where the god of this world, the prince of the power of the air rules. O believer, bless your covenant God afresh, that he has called you out of this darkness into his marvelous light, and has translated you into the kingdom of his dear Son! And why has he done this? Truly, that Christ should reign in your mind, that you should mind the things of Christ, and that you should enjoy all the blessings and comforts of his kingdom. Therefore, put on Christ your King—as the glory and comfort of your mind.

> *"This I say therefore, and testify in the Lord, that you henceforth walk not as other Gentiles walk, in the vanity of their mind— having the understanding dark-*

ened, being alienated from the life of God through the ignorance that is in them, because of the blindness of their heart" – Ephesians 4:17-18.

The vanity of the mind is our *fault* and our *shame* — and a chief cause of our misery. We too much mind earthly, carnal and sensual things. Christ our chief glory, is thus banished from, and kept out of our minds. Trifling, vain conversation, too much prevails among professors. This plainly reveals the vanity of the mind. When we can discern the hour of the day by the sundial, we know that the sun shines. When Christ the Sun of righteousness shines in the mind — the tongue, will how it is with the heart; and the life will manifest his glory. If we are living, loving Christians, we shall be very jealous over the workings of our minds, and be deeply concerned to keep them in a sweet, holy, humble, heavenly frame. This can only be done by putting on our beloved Christ in our minds. For, says Isaiah, "You will keep in perfect peace all who trust in you, whose *thoughts* are fixed on you!" (Isa. 26:3).

Our dear Lord says, "Where your treasure is, there will your heart be also" (Matt. 6:21). Is not Christ our richest treasure? Should he not be ever in our minds, and our minds ever on him? It is said of a Spanish ambassador, that when he saw the so-much cried up treasury of St. Mark in Venice, that he fell to groping in the chests and trunks. On being asked the reason, he said he was feeling whether they had a bottom. Said he, "My king's treasure in the mines of Mexico and Peru far exceeds yours; for they have no bottom; yours have." O Christian, the riches of your Christ are boundless and bottomless. You have in Christ, *unsearchable riches* — an inexhaustible treasure, which never fails!

How to Put On Christ in Our Minds

Then, imitate the miser. Let your mind dwell on your treasure. Let your treasure be ever uppermost in your mind. Is the miser's mind ever upon, and ever going out after his treasure? So let your minds dwell on Christ. Does he value himself by his treasure? So must you value yourself—upon Christ. Is he always poring over his precious wealth? So should you pour over your precious Christ. Does the miser love to inspect, and count over his beloved gold? So let your mind be ever inspecting your beloved Christ, in his wonderful person, as God and man; his amazing love, in laying down his life for you, his enemy, and his glorious salvation of you, an ungodly sinner. —Be constantly counting over all the great and precious promises which you have in him—and the graces, blessings, and comforts which you have from him, and the certain glory, which you soon shall enjoy with him! Is the miser careful to keep, and fearful of losing, any part of his possession? So let it be between Christ and your mind. Put him on. Hold him fast. Cleave to him. Be careful to enjoy him. Be ever fearful of losing any blessing or comfort he has promised to bestow. Thus put on Christ; thus clothe your mind with him as your treasure; let all your hopes center in him, and all your affections fix upon him. Now, even now, this very moment, the next and the next, yes, until moments are all fled, and time itself is swallowed up in eternity, be putting on Christ—receiving out of his inexhaustible fullness, grace upon grace, blessing upon blessing, comfort upon comfort. So put on Christ your treasure, as to count all things but dross and dung compared to him.

> *"I also consider everything to be a loss in view of the surpassing value of knowing Christ Jesus my Lord. Because of Him I have suffered the loss of all things and*

consider them filth, so that I may gain Christ!"
– Philippians 3:8

Put on Christ as the *glory* of your mind. O what thirst is there in our minds, after that phantom—the honors of this world! It was foretold to Agrippina, the mother of that cruel tyrant, Nero, that her son would be emperor, and afterwards kill her. Such was her thirst for her son's honor, that she replied, "Let but my son be emperor, then let him kill me, and spare not." O imitate her in the thirst after the glory of your mind. Well may you say, "Let my Christ be emperor. Let him but reign in my soul, and slay my thirst after all honor, but what comes from him." For, "Unto you who believe, Christ is precious, or rather an honor" (1 Pet. 2:7). Christ is precious and honorable in himself. Faith makes him peculiarly so to the mind. And it is the peculiar work of a believing mind, to be putting on Christ, and to exercise itself upon Christ, as its greatest honor, and chief glory. And he says, "Those who honor me, I will honor."

Consider, you have nothing but Christ to make you honorable in God's sight. As a sinner you are in the utmost disgrace in the court of heaven. You are a rebel against God. You dare not come into the presence of the King of kings. You have no proper clothing to appear in before him. You have nothing of your own but—filthy rags, which cannot hide your nakedness. So that you have nothing but fear and shame in yourself. But when you clothe your mind with Christ, who is your honor, what boldness does this inspire! For, he has dignified our nature, by taking it upon himself. Christ in our flesh has taken off the penalty of our rebellion. He has, in our flesh, wrought out a glorious righteousness for us to appear in before God. Yes, he has made us *kings* and *priests* unto God. He now stands pleading our cause before the throne of God. He pours upon us the graces of his Spirit. He makes us all glorious within, and puts on us clothing of wrought gold (Psa. 45:13) even the rich robe of righteousness. He brings us into the honorable relation of children of God; He makes us heirs of God; yes, co-heirs with himself, of God. He brings us into a state of adoption, as children of God—and pours upon us the Spirit of adoption, whereby we call God, "Abba, Father." What honor can be compared to this! Yet such honor have all Christ's saints.

Therefore, as all your honor comes by Christ, put him on in your mind as your greatest honor. Ever reflect on your new birth, and heavenly pedigree. Clothe your mind with what honor now comes to you by Christ, and what glory awaits you with him in the heavenly mansions. So you will look down with a holy contempt upon all objects beneath your Beloved.

Bless the Lord my soul, and raise
A glad and grateful song
To my dear Redeemer's praise;
For I to him belong.

He, my goodness, strength and God,
In whom I live, and move, and am,
Paid my ransom with his blood,
My portion is the Lamb.

Again—as to *pleasure*. Where, O Christian, can your mind fix for solid, lasting pleasure—but in the enjoyment of your Savior? Fables relate that, *Pleasure* went to bathe herself: having stripped off her clothes, and laid them by the water; *Sorrow* came, put them on and departed. Hence, say they, "the pleasures of this world are only sorrows in pleasure's garb." You have found it so. It will ever be so. But if Christ is put on, as the chief delight of the mind, we shall find pleasure arrayed in the garments of joy. "For in Christ's presence there is fullness of joy, and at his right hand there are pleasures for evermore" (Psa. 16:11). Put on Christ as the delight of your mind, and you shall be abundantly satisfied with him! He will make you drink of the river of his pleasures (Psa. 36:8).

Aristotle mentions a parcel of ground in Sicily, which sends forth such a strong smell of fragrant flowers, that no hounds can hunt near there, because their scent is so confounded by the sweet fragrance. Thus it will be, when Christ is put on the mind, as our chief pleasure; we shall find such sweet fragrance flowing from him, as will confound our scent, and prevent our hunting after the vain pleasures of sense, and the carnal joys of a wicked world. For says the living, loving spouse to Jesus her beloved bridegroom, "Your oils have a pleasing fragrance, Your name is like purified oil; Therefore the maidens love you." (Song 1:3). O there is such precious fragrance in the name of Christ, the anointed of God, to be our Jesus, our husband, redeemer, justifier and sanctifier—as perfumes the mind with joy, excites a holy love, and kills every unholy desire after all other pleasures—that are not to be found in him. Chaste virgins prefer the love of Christ to all other gratifications.

O Christian, can you cast in your lot with the spiritually dead – to partake of their diversions? Can you hunt after them? Can your mind find delight and pleasure in them? If so, be assured you are not a chaste virgin to Christ. You go after other lovers beside him. You have put off Christ from your mind, as your only and chief object for joy and pleasure. Thy Lord finds no pleasure in your ways. Your mind finds no pleasure in him. Is it any marvel then, if instead of sweet joy in the Lord, you find dejecting doubts, and distressing fears racking your mind? For you have fallen under that severe and cutting reproof from the Lord, "My people have committed two evils: They have forsaken me, the fountain of living waters, and hewed out cisterns for themselves, broken cisterns that can hold no water" (Jer 2:13). O bewail your foolishness of folly, and your basest ingratitude! Cry to the Holy Spirit, to take of the things of Christ, and to show them unto you afresh—so as to enamor your heart, and captivate your affections; that with David you may say, "Return again to your rest, O my soul, for the Lord has dealt bountifully with you" (Psa. 116:7). Put on the Lord Jesus Christ—as the only love, and chief delight of your mind. For he said: "I have formed you, you are My servant; I have blotted out, like a thick cloud, your transgressions, and like a cloud, your sins. Return to Me, for I have redeemed you" (Isa. 44:21-22). "Return, O faithless children, declares the LORD; for I am your master. "Return, you backsliding children, and I will heal your faithlessness" (Jer. 3:14-22).

> *How great the Christian's portion is!*
> *What heaps of joy, what worlds of bliss,*
>   *The Lord for them prepares!*
> *Their boundless treasures who can know?*
> *For all above, and all below,*
>   *And God, and Christ are theirs!*

Chapter 5

How to Put On Christ
In Our Memory

When Alexander had conquered Darius king of Persia, among the spoils, he found a rich cabinet of the choicest jewels. After some thought, what to use it for, Alexander concluded, that as the works of Homer were his greatest delight, he would lay them up in that rich cabinet. O you Christ-conquered soul—is not Christ your chief joy? Are not his works your greatest delight? Then, put on Christ; lay up his glorious work of salvation in the rich cabinet of your soul—your memory. Let your memory be the ark to contain your Savior! There, like the virgin mother, lay up, keep and ponder upon your dear Lord and his precious sayings.

Many complain of bad memories. They cannot remember many things. They cannot retain things long. Here then is the one thing needful. Here is but one short, gospel work for your memory. "Remember, that Jesus Christ was raised up from the dead" (2 Tim. 2:8). Exercise your memory upon this. Clothe your memory with this. For this finishing stroke includes the whole of your Lord's blessed and joyful works, from his birth in the ignoble stable, until his ascension to his kingdom in glory. Clothe your memory constantly with the joy of this—that the eternal Son of the eternal Father became an infant of days, lived to be a man of years, died as an accursed malefactor bearing our sins—the *guilt* of our sins, the *curse* of our sins, all the *wrath* due to our sins, and all the *penalties* which our sins deserved, in his own body on the tree! Remember that he, the true scapegoat, carried all our sins away into the land of forgetfulness.

Hence thus says your God and Father, "Your sins, and your iniquities, I will remember no more" (Jer. 31:34). "Though your sins and your iniquities be sought for—they shall not be found" (Jer. 1:20). You cannot—but at times remember your sins. It is fitting that you should, to humble you, and to cause you to remember the love of Jesus, who bore them, suffered for them, and has taken them all away. O then remember that Jesus was raised again from the dead. He left all your sins buried in his sepulcher. He rose again without them. You are forever justified from them. God does not remember them against you. He imputed them to your surety and he imputes to you his righteousness. There is no condemnation against you for your sins.

Here is blessed joyful work for your memory. No matter what you forget, if you do but remember this. Put on Christ in your memory. Ever remember him—who always remembers you. Clothe your memory with his love, who loved you from eternity, became your surety in time, was clothed with your sins and your curses as with a garment; that he might clothe you with the precious robe of his everlasting righteousness, and adorn your soul with the graces of his Holy Spirit! He bids us, "remember Lot's wife," (Luke 17:32), that we may never look back from him—but ever look to him, that we so be turned into pillars of love; and that the smoke of the incense of praise might ever ascend to him! When you find sadness and distress of soul, what is the reason for it? The prophet tells you, "There shall be desolation, because you have *forgotten* the God of your salvation, and have not been *mindful* of the rock of your strength" (Isa. 17:9,10). O see the evil, and apply the remedy.

When Cyrus captured the king of Armenia, his son Tigranes, and their wives and children prisoners; upon their humble submission, beyond their hopes, he gave them all their liberty and lives. On their return home, they all highly commended Cyrus—some for his person, some for his power, and some for his mercy. Tigranes asked his wife, "What do you think of Cyrus? Is he not a noble person, of majestic presence and greatest mercy?" "Truly" said she, "I know not what manner of person he is—I did not look at him." "No!" said he, "where were your eyes? Upon whom did you look?" "Why," said she, "I fixed my eyes wholly on you—my mind was wholly intent on you, for I heard what I shall never forget from you; when with such affection to me, you voluntarily offered to lay down your life for my ransom."

O Christian, upon whom should your eyes, your mind, your memory, be ever wholly fixed—but on your matchless husband, the lovely, and ever loving Jesus—who so freely laid down his life for your ransom? Imitate the church, who says of her beloved, "We will be glad and rejoice in you." Why? because "We will remember your love" (Song 1:4). It is the memory of Christ's love, which causes gladness of heart, and joy of soul. O how wonderful is the love of Christ to us! O remember his love, in betrothing us to himself in eternity—in espousing us to himself in time, that he might "dwell in our hearts by faith, that being rooted and grounded in love, we may be able to comprehend with all saints, what is the breadth, and length, and depth, and height, and may know the love of Christ which passes knowledge; that we may be filled with all the fullness of God" (Eph. 3:17, etc.). All the fullness of God dwells in Christ. If Christ dwells in you by faith, you have all the fullness of God's love dwelling in you. Remember this, and be joyful.

> *O, to grace, what mighty debtors,*
> *Daily, hourly, Lord, are we!*
> *Let that grace, like strongest fetters,*
> *Bind our wandering hearts to thee.*
> *Prone to wander, Lord we feel them:*
> *Prone to leave you, God of love,*
> *Here's our hearts – O take and seal them,*
> *Seal them from your courts above.*

Chapter 6

How to Put On Christ
In Our Conscience

I have read of one who undertook to make a fat sheep lean, and yet allow it daily a sufficient quantity of wholesome food, soft and easy lodging, and security from all danger, that nothing should hurt it. This he effected, by putting the sheep into an iron grate, and placing a ravenous wolf nearby in another, who was always howling and scratching to come at the poor sheep. This sad sound and worse sight, so terrified the sheep, that he had little joy to sleep, and less to eat, so that his flesh soon decreased, and he became very lean.

Just so, Satan, that wolf of prey, serves many of Christ's sheep. He accuses, teases, and terrifies their poor consciences. When they cry for peace, he says to the poor sinner, as Jehu said to the messengers of Joram, "What have you to do with peace?" Though Christ is set before the sinner, as his food, his clothing, and for the peace of his conscience, yet what with listening to Satan's lies, and the prevailings of unbelief, the soul neglects to feed on Christ, and put him on for peace of conscience: therefore he grows very lean, and lives very uncomfortably. But what dishonor is this to the glorious work of Christ! And what distress of conscience do many of his beloved sheep thus labor under!

But why should it be so with any of us? Has not our good shepherd laid down his life for his sheep? Has not the work of Christ, in his life and death for them, perfectly satisfied the justice of God? Has not his resurrection from the dead fully declared it? Is not the court of heaven fully satisfied with what Christ has done and suffered for us? Are these facts, or are they fables? If we really believe them, can we want more to satisfy our conscience, and to give us peace? The death and resurrection of Christ is sufficient to bring peace, to the conscience of the greatest sinner out of hell. Yes, these facts will most assuredly possess that sinner with peace, who puts on this blessed truth in his conscience. And by maintaining this truth in the conscience, peace with God will be preserved. Therefore, at all times, when you see your sins, and are considering what a miserable sinner you are, put on once again the life and death of the Son of God in your *conscience*, as the greatest, most precious, and most comfortable truth in the world.

There is no other way for you to obtain peace of conscience. O how blessed and joyful to have the answer of a *good* conscience towards God! Peter tells us plainly how we possess this. Is it because we can answer all the demands of God's holy law, and say we have perfectly fulfilled it? No, this is the answer of an *ignorant* conscience. Is it because we can answer to God, that we are not sinners, that we have no sin? No, this is the answer of a *lying* conscience. But the answer of a good conscience towards God comes by this, and no other way than this, "by the resurrection of Jesus Christ, who is gone into heaven, and is on the right hand of God" (1 Pet. 3:21,22). There, says Paul, "He now "appears in the presence of God *for us*" (Heb. 9:24).

Now, my fellow sinner, who, like me, was as a sheep going astray—but have now returned to the Shepherd and Guardian of our souls—act up to your high-calling, and exalted privilege. Put on the Lord Jesus Christ in your conscience. Be daily, be constantly, holding the mystery of faith in a pure conscience. What is this mystery of faith? It is most marvelous and astonishing. While angels are prying into it, sinners—vile, miserable, yes, the very chief of sinners, are enjoying the comfort of it! What are you and I but sinners? An accusing devil, and unbelief, can make of us nothing more than sinners. Yet this precious mystery of faith is to be held in our consciences, that though we are in ourselves, sin-accused, law-condemned, hopeless, helpless, ruined, lost and desperate sinners; yet in Christ Jesus we are justified from all sin, freed from all condemnation, restored to the love, favor and image of God, are at peace with God, saved in thr Lord with an everlasting salvation, and have a hope full of immortality. Well may we cry out in wonder and amazement, "What has the amazing grace of God wrought! What has the precious love of Christ effected!" Truly, a salvation which super-abounds all the aboundings of sin!

Now it is by holding this mystery of faith in our consciences, that we become true worshipers of God, and have no more conscience of sin to our condemnation. Our hearts are sprinkled by Christ's blood from an evil or guilty conscience (Heb. 10:2). And our consciences are purged from dead works to serve the living God (Heb.

9:9). O precious work of putting on the Lord Jesus Christ in our conscience! O joyful exercise, of holding fast the mystery of faith in a pure conscience!

But ever remember, you have a most subtle and powerful enemy, who will by every wile, stratagem and device, aim to oppose you in this blessed work! Be on your guard against him. Satan is called our enemy — "Be careful! Watch out for attacks from the Devil, *your great enemy*. He prowls around like a roaring lion, looking for some victim to devour!" (1 Pet. 5:8). He was an avowed enemy to the work of Christ *for* us; and he is a powerful adversary to that peace, comfort, joy and holiness, which arises from the work of Christ in us. He continually prowls around like a roaring lion, looking for some victim to devour! Though he is not allowed to *destroy* our souls, yet he will rage and roar, and strive by all means to disturb our peace, and destroy our comfort in Christ. Therefore he will tempt and accuse, if by any means he can fix the sense of sin, guilt and condemnation upon our consciences.

Now there is but one way to Satan's devices. This is it: "Resist him steadfastly in the faith." (1 Pet. 5:9).

What is this—but to put on Christ in our conscience—to wrap ourselves in what Christ has done for us, and is to us? In the faith of this, resist every attack of Satan. Does he accuse of sin? Hold up your shield of faith, your redemption in the blood of Christ, even the forgiveness of all your sins—the blood of Christ cleanses from all sin before God. It was blood shed by a holy Savior, and accepted by a righteous Judge. This will "quench all the fiery darts" of your enemy. This calms the terrors of conscience and brings peace. Here is the witness of the Spirit. "There is no condemnation from God against you, for you are in Christ Jesus" (Rom 8:1).

Does Satan accuse you, that you are a sinner before God, and cursed by the law of God? The charge is just: own it. Yet this need not destroy your peace of conscience. Put on Christ, your breastplate of righteousness. "For he was made sin for us, that we sinners might be made the righteousness of God in him" (2 Cor. 5:21). "Christ has redeemed us from the curse of the law, being made a curse for us." (Gal. 3:13). By him, all who believe are justified, fully discharged, and perfectly acquitted "from *all* things" (Acts 13:19). Though sin has "reigned unto death", yet grace "reigns through the righteousness of Jesus Christ our Lord, unto eternal life" (Rom. 5:21). Now, why is Christ, his grace, and righteousness, thus held forth to us in scripture? Surely it is, that we should so put him on in our consciences as to answer every demand of law and justice, silence every accusation of Satan, possess peace and joy in God, knowing assuredly that we have eternal life in Christ. O this living and abiding in the Lord, is precious! It is living like ourselves, children of God, members of Christ, and heirs of glory.

For Satan can stand against all that we are in ourselves, bring accusations against all our works and doings, and thereby distress our consciences. But we are complete in Christ. His perfect work is our shield of faith, with which we quench all the fiery darts of the wicked one, and obtain perfect victory over him. With this shield we are to defend our conscience against every attack; so shall we, in the experience of faith, joyfully sing, "Now has come salvation and strength, and the kingdom of God, and the power of Christ; for our accuser is cast down, and overcome by the blood of the Lamb, and by the word of the testimony of our dear Savior's atonement, righteousness and salvation" (Rev. 12:10-11). He is overcome by the blood of the Lamb, and by the word of the testimony of our dear Saviour's atonement, righteousness and salvation

But Satan not only accuses for sin—but tempts to sin; and often injects the most horrible thoughts into the mind. This need not distress our conscience. Why should it? For temptations are not sins. Ten thousand temptations can bring no guilt upon the conscience. As to horrid injections, Satan shall answer for them—not us. Our Lord "was in all points tempted like us, yet without sin." Tempted sinners should remember this, and look to their once tempted Savior. To him they should flee for grace to stand, and power to conquer. So shall we ever prove that "we are more than conquerors through Christ who has loved us".

O see to it then, that you do not give place to the enemy, no, not for one moment! Having such an armor for our conscience, as precious Christ, his rich grace, his perfect righteousness, his glorious salvation, let us clothe our conscience with this, for victory and for peace. Our very doubts and fears are enemies to the glory of our Lord, and the peace of our consciences. But seeing we have such a glorious Savior, such a finished salvation, and are complete in him—why should these so prevail in us? When they do, it is because you do not give Christ the pre-eminence in your conscience. You do not firmly believe, and constantly live upon, this sin-subduing and soul-sanctifying truth, "If any man sins, we have an advocate with the Father, Jesus Christ the righteous, and he is the atoning sacrifice for our sins" (1 John 2:1,2). "The blood of Jesus purifies us from all sin!" (1 John 1:7). Both from before God, and in our own consciences. "And we are made the righteousness of God in him" (2 Cor. 5:21).

Dr. Sibbs says, "This is the main point in religion, and the comfort of Christians, to be lost in themselves, and to be only found in Christ, not having their own righteousness, but the righteousness of God *in* him. This is a mystery which none know but a believing soul; none see corruption more; none see themselves freed more. They have an *inward* sight to see corruption, and an *inward* faith to see God reconciled. And there can be no greater honor to Christ than this, in the sense of sin, of wants, imperfections, stains, and blemishes, to wrap ourselves in the righteousness of Christ with boldness, to go clothed in the garments of our elder Brother to the throne of grace. This is an honor to Christ, to attribute so much to his righteousness that being clothed therewith, we can boldly break through the fire of God's justice, and all those terrible attributes, when we see them all satisfied in Christ; for Christ with his righteousness could go through the justice of God, having satisfied it to the full for us. And we being clothed with his righteousness and satisfaction, may go through too. It is the character of a judicious, believing, Christian soul to value the righteousness of Christ out of himself, laboring, living and dying, to appear in that."

God's precious word is the best remedy against all doubts and fears. The only antidote against unbelief is the truth as it is in Jesus. In believing this we shall be filled with all peace and joy of conscience, and abound in hope, through the power of the Holy Spirit (Rom. 15:13). And the God of peace shall bruise Satan under your feet shortly (Rom. 16:20).

The Believer's Pocket Companion

Cease your fears then, weak believer,
*   Jesus Christ is still the same,*
Yesterday, today, forever,
*   Savior is his blessed name!*

Lowliness of heart and meekness,
*   To the bleeding Lamb belong;*
Trust in him, and by your weakness,
*   You shall prove that Christ is strong.*

Chapter 7

Why We Should
Put On Christ

Why put on Christ? Truly, because without the enjoyment of him we cannot draw one comfortable breath, live one happy moment, nor take one delightful step in the road of life, towards certain death, and an eternal world. A real Christian, of all men is the most miserable—if his *mind*, *memory*, and *conscience*, do not possess his beloved Christ, his precious love, covenant grace, and finished salvation. Therefore consider,

First, *"Put on the Lord Jesus Christ,"* is a command to you, O believers. Though it is not under the form of a legal command, "Do this and live. Fulfill this and be saved." yet it is a command under the law of faith, by which all divine comfort is enjoyed, and all human boasting is excluded. It is a command of covenant grace and love, to you, believers, who are alive to God through Jesus Christ, and are already accepted, pardoned, justified, and saved in Christ. Paul gives this command from the Holy Spirit, the glorifier of Jesus, and the comforter of his members; that by constantly obeying it, we may be comfortable in our minds, more humble in our heart, more holy in life, and more comfortable in our souls. Therefore think not lightly of it. But ever consider yourself bound, by all the sacred ties of covenant grace and love, to obey this gospel command. As Aaron's rod swallowed up all the rods of Pharaoh's sorcerers, so does this command swallow up and include in it, all other commands. If love is the fulfilling of the whole law, putting on Christ is fulfilling the whole of the law, and of the gospel. The servants of Naaman said to him, "If the prophet had bid you do some great thing, would you not have done it? How much rather when he says to you, Wash and be clean?" So when the apostle says to you, O believer, put on the Lord Jesus Christ, and be happy in your mind, joyful in your memory, and peaceful in your conscience, will you not do it? O ever consider this as the one thing needful. The work is yours. The power to do it is from the Lord.

Secondly, your daily experience teaches the necessity of putting on Christ. This command is suited to your fallen state, as you are a naked, indigent, hopeless, helpless, unholy sinner in yourself—as well as to your being a regenerate soul, a new creature, a believer in Christ. Some have got such vast high notions of believers, as though they were not still sinners. Hence they cannot endure the phrase, believing sinners—saved sinners. But let experience determine this matter. I will venture to assert, that if you do not see yourself a sinner, from day to day, you are not a believer of the truth. No, if you do not see that you are naked, indigent, hopeless, helpless, sinner, too, you do not know yourself even as you are known. *Sin* is not exceeding sinful to you. *Self* is not humbled and loathed by you. *Christ* is not most precious in your eyes. Yet, though sin dwells in us, it does not have dominion over us. It cannot; for we are not under the law, which only pronounces the curse of sin; but under the grace of Christ, which actually subdues the power of sin (Rom. 6:14).

Though a believer in Christ, you are still a *naked* sinner in yourself. You have no righteousness of your own which you have wrought out, which can screen you from divine justice, answer all the demands of God's law, and entitle you to his favor. Your own righteousness is no better than filthy rags, too ragged to hide your shame; too filthy to endure the piercing eye of God's purity; but must be burnt up by the fire of his justice. True, in Christ you have an infinitely perfect, and everlastingly glorious righteousness, to appear in before God. But it is as true, you can only enjoy the comfort of this, by putting on Christ in your mind, memory and conscience. And it is equally true, unless you see, notwithstanding all your works, duties and performances, the graces of the Spirit in you, and the fruits of righteousness produced by you, that you are still that naked sinner, who must be found in Christ, and clothed with his righteousness, or you cannot be justified before God — but must be eternally condemned for sin. Unless you see this you will see no need to put on Christ. But the Holy Spirit convinces us of sin, causes us to see that we are stripped of all by sin, and keeps up the sight of our nakedness, on purpose that we should put on Christ, that in the experience of faith we may say with the church: "I will greatly rejoice in the Lord, *my* soul shall be joyful in my God, for he has clothed *me* with the garments of salvation, he has covered *me* with the robe of righteousness" (Isa. 61:10). O then, bless the Spirit, for eyes to see your nakedness. Under every sight of it, put on Christ, that you may glory in him, who is *the Lord Our Righteousness*.

Again, Though a believer in Christ, yet you are *indigent* in yourself. There is not a more poor, needy, indigent thing in creation, than you are, and see yourself in the light of truth to be. You behold a total lack in yourself of everything that is good. You see what an infinite debt you owe to law and justice, and you have not one farthing to discharge it! No, nor ever will you have a farthing to pay. No, more; every day, you are running farther and farther in debt. You cannot but think a reckoning day must come. Under these views, fear and distress must haunt you. The dread of being eternally shut up in the prison of hell, must terrify you. What can you do under such circumstances, but put on your blessed surety, Christ! What, but answer every demand of law and justice, with his dying words, *it is finished*, the debt is discharged, the creditor is satisfied! You well please with Christ, and He with you. Record this afresh in your mind and memory, that conscience may take the comfort, and the Lord have all the glory.

Away then with your dejected heart and gloomy countenance. Live up to your joyful privilege. Will you grovel in poverty, groan in wretchedness, pine with need, grapple with misery, and be burdened with distress? What! when you know the grace of our Lord Jesus, who for our sakes became poor, that we through his poverty might be made rich? Then, under the sense of deepest indigence, put on Christ, in whom you have unsearchable riches. This is the humble teaching of faith — to know that in ourselves, we have nothing. This is the joyful experience of faith — to know that in Christ we possess all things. O rest not without the comfort of this. Love, bless, and glory in your divine surety. And in the felt sense of your own weakness, be daily leaning upon your

Beloved. So will you be safely, sweetly, and comfortably, coming up out of the wilderness of this world, singing,

> *How blessed am I, whose heart is set,*
> *To find the way to Zion's gate!*
> *Christ is my strength, and thro' the road*
> *I'll lean upon my helper, God.*

Once more. Though a believer in Christ, yet you are in yourself a *hopeless sinner*; therefore you should put on Christ, who is our hope, that your soul may be strong, lively, and joyful in hope. What! Though I have been in Christ so many years, and in self a hopeless sinner still? What! Do I have nothing in *self* to cast the anchor of hope upon? No! What, cast the anchor within the ship to hold it? Ridiculous! True, the grace of hope is in the heart. But the object of hope is Christ. The anchor of hope is cast into the wide ocean of God's love to sinners in Christ. O the working of that legal spirit, which is ever seeking the pride of self, wanting to entertain a good opinion of ourselves and to have something within ourselves to trust in, and in which to glory! This spirit opposes the glory of Christ, and keeps us from putting on Christ, as our only hope, and chief glory.

Hence it is, our hearts so often sink, when our comforts forsake us. For hope in self will soon give up the ghost. It may live just while the sunshine of a warm state lasts. But let the north wind blow, let but a cloud arise in the mind, a fresh sense of sin spring up in the memory, or a little storm of corruption rage in the conscience—and *hope in self* will wither like Jonah's gourd. Hence we see so many professors so fluctuating and wavering. Now they are all light, joy and peace. Then they are all darkness, distress and terror. Do not you experience something of this at times? Why is it? Because you inclined to something in *yourself* as your hope, and decline from Christ, who is emphatically called "our hope"(1 Tim. 1:1). Therefore he is to be constantly put on — and wholly lived upon — as the only hope of us hopeless sinners!

Brethren, consider your calling. It is with faithful Abraham, who "Against all hope, Abraham in hope believed." For all in nature and self, is hopeless. Yes, there is nothing but despair in us. We have the sentence of death in ourselves, that we should not trust in ourselves. Sin, death and despair are written upon all we are — and upon all we do. We find one indwelling sin, lust and corruption after another — rise in us. Just as with David; first a bear attacks him, then a lion, next a giant; and then a king, and then the Philistines war against him. Why all this? to exercise his arms, and call forth his hope in his Lord. Why are such powerful enemies — such as brutish lusts, raging corruptions, gigantic unbelief, potent carnal reasonings — left in us after conversion? All are to put us out of a high esteem of ourselves, to drive us out of all hope in ourselves, and to cause us to put on Christ, our hope. Thus, "Experience works hope" (Rom. 5:4). We are always to be fighting and conflicting with hopeless self. Therefore we have continual need to put on Christ, that we may be lively and comfortable in the sweet experience of *Christ in us the hope of glory* (Col. 1:27).

Farther; though a believer in Christ, yet you are a *helpless* sinner in yourself. "What!" say some, "a converted person, a believer, a child of God — and yet a helpless sinner?" Yes! Infancy itself is not more helpless in natural things, than a believer is in spiritual things. Where then is the difference between a believer and an unbeliever? Essentially in this. The latter is insensible of his own weakness, therefore proudly boasts in, and vainly glories of his own strength. He is under this malediction, "Cursed is the man who makes flesh his arm," for, "his heart departs from the Lord" (Jer. 17:5). But the believer knows and feels, that he is not of himself sufficient to think or do anything of himself. He sees constant need of being strengthened by the Spirit's might in the inner man. For blessed is the man who trusts in the Lord; whose hope the Lord is. "But do we not grow stronger in ourselves, and find more help and power from ourselves, to withstand our enemies, to fight our good fight, to run our race, and to perfect holiness?" No! If we think so, it is plain that we are not growing up into Christ—but growing down into self. If the Lord has given me to know anything of this matter, after being upwards of twenty years in Christ, I freely declare, that I find myself to be, just that weak, helpless sinner I was when I first came to Jesus with, "Lord help me! Lord save me—or I perish!" I find myself more helpless now—than I thought myself then. I see more constant need to put on Christ, and to say, surely in *the Lord* I have strength (Isa. 45:24).

I never more firmly believed than now, this truth of my Lord, "Without me you can do nothing" (John 15:5). Never, never did I see less cause to trust in my own strength; never so much need to hear and obey my Lord when he says, "Let him who glories, glory in this, that he understands and knows me, that I am the Lord, who exercises loving-kindness, judgment and righteousness in the earth" (Jer. 9:24). O to understand and know this exercise of the loving-kindness of my Lord, to me—a weak, helpless, vile sinner, is the glory and rejoicing of my soul.

Well—but here is the poor helpless sinner, surrounded with enemies on every side—without and within—called to fight the Lord's battles against the world, the flesh, and the devil—called to perform duties—to exercise graces—to bear his Lord's cross, and to follow him in the regeneration, can he do all this in his own strength? Certainly not! And blessed be our covenant God—we are not left to our helpless selves! He has put precious faith in our hearts. As Jesus is its author, so he is its object. As faith comes from him, it leads the soul out of nature and self—to the him who created all things. Therefore this is the work of the believing soul, "I will lift up my eyes unto the hills, from whence comes my help." Here is the *exercise* of faith. "My help comes from the Lord, who has made heaven and earth" (Psa. 121:1,2). Here is the *experience* of faith. What Lord made heaven and earth? Truly, that Jehovah-Jesus, whom you are exhorted to put on. John expressly tells us so: "*all things* were made by him, and without him was not anything made that was made" (John 1:3).

Eternal praise to you, O blessed Spirit, for this your witness, to our Immanuel's eternal power and godhead. Eternal thanks to you, O loving Father, that you have laid help upon one who is mighty, for those who have no might in themselves; and has exalted one chosen out of the people, to be the help of those sinners who find no help in themselves. Eternal blessings be on you, O Son of God, for, though we have destroyed ourselves, yet you have lovingly assured us, "in *me* is your help found" (Hos. 13:9). O gracious Spirit, enable me to make it my daily work, constant duty, chief privilege, and grand concern—to clothe my mind, memory, and conscience, with this joyful truth—that Christ, *my Lord* and *my God*, is my help and my shield, against the face of every enemy!

In the faith of this, well may I bid defiance to all my foes, smile at their number, defy their power, shout "vic-

Why We Should Put On Christ

tory!" in every attack, and in triumph cry out, "I am more than conqueror through Christ who has loved me!"

When Alexander came against a people who dwelt on the rocks, they smiled at his approach, and bid defiance to his power, boldly saying, "unless your soldiers can fly in the air, we fear you not; we are safe; our defense is impregnable!" So, O my soul, dwelling in Christ the rock of your salvation, you are safe and secure from every foe. "For you dwell on high, and your defense shall be the munitions of rocks" (Isa. 33:16).

What though you find and feel, from hour to hour, that you have "no power of yourself to help yourself," in forcing any enemy, in subduing one sin, in mortifying one lust, in exercising one grace, or in performing one duty—be not discouraged. Paul was as helpless in himself as you are, yet he said, "I can do all things." So may you, by the very same means as he did, "through Christ who strengthens me" (Phil. 4:13). To begin well, is to end well. Begin with Christ; put him on as your strength, so shall you end every work to his glory. O this is sweet and pleasant walking, "I will go in the strength of the Lord God; will make mention of your righteousness, even of yours alone" (Psa. 71:16).

Put on Christ—for though a justified, sanctified believer in him, yet, in yourself, you are an unholy sinner. Your nature is earthly, your desires are sensual, and your tempers are devilish. In your flesh dwells no good thing. Out of it proceeds all manner of evil. Therefore you have no holiness—but what you have in Christ, and derive from him. Here is the decree of heaven, "Without holiness—personal holiness of heart, lip and life—no man shall see the Lord" (Heb. 12:14). This is the declaration of covenant grace, "Christ of God is made unto us sanctification" (1 Cor. 1:30). See the glory of gospel grace. You are not left to labor to get holiness to sanctify you—but you are sanctified in *Christ,* and you are to put him on, for the subduing your lusts, mortifying your corruptions, softening and sweetening your tempers—so will you comfortably go on, perfecting holiness in the fear of God.

For while vital union to Christ, and holy communion with Christ, are sensibly maintained in the mind, memory and conscience—we shall keep chaste to him; we shall keep our vessel in sanctification to his honor; and though sin be not dead in us—yet we shall be dead to sin. It will lose all its mighty charms in our eyes. We shall detest the very appearance of evil. And all the pleasures of sense will be under our feet. Clothed with Christ the new man, we shall put off the old man with his deeds: and our one chief aim will be—to please Christ in all things. O study this point deeply. To be holy is to be like God. The more Christ is put on, the more holiness in life and walk; the more holiness, the more enjoyment of God, the more assurance of being a child of God, and of eternally enjoying the presence of God. You will ever find this true in experience, that when Christ is put on within, as the peace, comfort and joy of the heart—all that is contrary to holiness will be put off in the life.

Thirdly, Why should we put on Christ?—Because we are called by our Lord to deny ourselves, and to follow him. But if Christ is not put on within, we shall have little heart, and little power, to follow him in the life. Never was the gospel more adorned than it is in our day—if fine clothing and elegant dress may be said to adorn it! Never had Christ more followers than now—if professors may be said to follow him, who can gratify themselves in the vain pleasures and fashionable diversions of a sinful age. Alas! Such things tend to deprave the mind, manifest its vanity, drive Christ from the memory, and are quite opposite to all self-denial and holy obedience. Besides, how sadly is money lavished away in these things—while many of Christ's saints are in need of common necessaries! O how can such answer for it to their Lord!

A beggar asked alms of a pious lady. She gave him six-pence, saying, "That is more than ever God gave me." "O" said the beggar, "say not so, Madam, for you have great wealth, and God gave you all." "No," replied she, "I speak the truth. God has not given—but *lent* me what I have, that I might bestow it on such as you. I am only the Lord's steward, and must give an account to him." O that this was more considered.

One can just as soon conceive, that a devil can be happy in the flames of hell—as that a child of God can seek for and find happiness at the play-house, the card-table, or any carnal diversions—while the love of Christ is warm upon his mind, his sorrows and sufferings of Christ are fresh in his memory, the sprinkling of the blood of Christ is felt upon his conscience, and the peace of God is ruling in his soul. Can those who give up themselves to vain things have never known the power and comfort of Christ's love? If they have, they must in a sense, have put off Christ, lost the feeling conviction of sin, of abstaining from the very appearance of evil, and of the absolute necessity of taking up their cross and following him. For if their minds were exercised in putting on Christ, the vanity of external adornments would fall off like leaves in autumn, their thirst after foolish pleasures would be quenched by Christ, the living water, and holy fellowship with Christ would cause them to put off their former conversation, the old man, which is corrupt according to the deceitful lusts. Fleshly lusts and Christ's love can never reign in one heart.

Oh then put on Christ, and you will deny yourself, and follow the Lord. You will be armored against the lust of the flesh, the lust of the eye, and the pride of life. Instead of your mind going out after lying vanities and deceitful pleasures, you will be swallowed up in God. Your memory will be taken up with the things which are freely given us of God. Your conscience will be peaceful in the love of your covenant God in Christ. Your life will be devoted to the glory of God your Father; and your study will be, not to live to the lusts of men—but to the will of God. For if Christ is in your mind and memory, your conscience will be tender; it will fear and abhor the very appearance of evil, and excite you to all holy obedience. Here appears the essential difference between *professing* and *possessing* Christ. The former will leave a man alive to self, and dead to Christ. The latter will make him dead to self, and alive to Christ.

Hence, in opposition to living after the flesh, and making provision for the flesh, to fulfill the lusts thereof, Paul does not teach like a heathen philosopher, or exhort like our modern moral preachers, to put on such a virtue, and to put off such a vice. But, says he, there is but this one way to put on all virtues, and to put off all vices. *"Put on the Lord Jesus Christ."* Christ is the only way, at once, to put on, all that is contrary to his precious love, our holy faith, and joyful hope, will assuredly be put off. Christ is the one thing needful. Let it be your one business, to put him on more and more!

When Pompey, by all his arguments and persuasions, could not keep his soldiers from going out of the camp, he laid himself down in the narrow passage which led out of it, saying, "Now go out if you will; but if you do, you shall trample upon your general." This overcame them. Not one would stir. We cannot go out of the camp of Christ into unlawful pleasures and sensual diversions, without, trampling underfoot the Son of God. O think of this! The Rabbis used to tell their pupils that sin made God's head ache. This we are sure of, sin pained the Son of God to the very soul. When you think of your sin—of the precious love, and dreadful sufferings of Christ for your sins—and put him on, it will cause you cheerfully to deny yourself, and delightfully to follow Jesus in the regeneration.

Fourthly, why should we put on Christ? Because it is the will of God our Father. "In this was manifested the love of God towards us, because God sent his only begotten Son into the world, that we might live through him" (1 John 4:9). And thus it is manifest, that we are the obedient children of God, receiving, putting on and living upon the Son of God. For to the praise of the glory of God's grace, he has made us accepted in his beloved Son (Eph. 1:6). O believer, consider this. Let your heart rejoice in this. Let your mind dwell on this. Record this in your memory, that your conscience may be peaceful, happy and comfortable in the view that though a sinner in yourself, yet you are acceptable to God, and perfectly accepted by him, in His son your elder brother; to the glory of God's rich, free, and abundant grace. It pleased the Father that in Christ all fullness should dwell. To what end? Even this joyful one, that we should live upon him, and out of this we should receive grace upon grace—until grace is swallowed up in glory!

O then, attend constantly to the voice of your heavenly Father. He calls in most tender love and affection, "Behold my elect, in whom my soul delights" (Isa. 42:1). And again, "This is my beloved Son in whom I am well pleased, *hear him*" (Matt. 17:5). What is implied in this call to behold Christ, and to hear him? It is as though our heavenly Father said thus to us, "My dear children, whom I love with an everlasting love, I would have you to be both holy and happy. For this end I gave my beloved Son to you. He is the one and only object, I would have you to fix your constant attention upon. Let your mind be turned away from all other objects to him. Behold him as *the Lord your Righteousness*. Let the ear of your soul ever attend his pleasing voice. Hear him, speaking in righteousness, mighty to save. So behold, so hear him, as to clothe your minds, memories and consciences, with the perfect atonement, which he has made for your sins—his perfect obedience to the law, as your righteousness, which he has wrought out for your justification—and with the glorious work which he has finished for your salvation. Put on my beloved Son as your priest, who died for your sins, and ever lives to pray for you—as your *mediator* to bless you—your *righteousness* to justify you—your *holiness* to sanctify you—your *redemption* to glorify you—and until you get to glory, as your *king* to reign in you, and to conquer for you! For I have given him as a covenant to you. In and from him you shall receive all the blessings of my everlasting love. In him you shall enjoy my peace which passes all understanding. This shall keep your hearts and minds in the knowledge and love of me, and in sweet fellowship with my beloved Son Jesus Christ."

O let us then obey our Father, by beholding, hearing, and putting on his beloved Son, as his most free and inestimably precious gift to sinners. For our Lord says, "the Father himself loves you, because you have loved me" (John 16:27).

Fifthly, we should put on Christ, for this is his own will concerning us. He gave himself for us, that he might be all in all to us—our food to nourish us, and our drink to refresh us. He says, "My flesh is food indeed, and my blood is drink indeed." He lived to be our righteousness to clothe us. He died for our sins, to save us. He lives again to comfort us. Therefore he says, "abide in me." "Continue in my love" (John 15:4,9). What does he mean? Truly, that we should always clothe our minds with his precious love, ever remember it, and ever exercise our conscience upon the wonders of his free, unmerited, unchangeable love to us. Thus let us ever abide in him, cleave to him, believe on him, so as to derive fresh power, peace and joy from him, that we may be constantly bringing forth fruit to his honor and glory.

Christ is continually calling us, "Hear and your souls shall live" (Isa. 55:3). Live by his word of grace and truth —live upon his blood and righteousness—live in the comfort of a pardoned, justified, sanctified state—live in a peaceful state—live in the joyful memory of his love and salvation—live, having our hearts sprinkled from an evil conscience by his blood—and live upon all the fullness of grace which is in him, receiving out of his fullness grace upon grace, until faith is lost in sight, hope in fruition, and love in the full enjoyment of Christ, in the realms of bliss and glory.

But are our minds at any time distressed with a sense of our sins, lusts and corruptions? Are our memories burdened, and our consciences heavy laden with these? What are we to do in this case? Do? Why remember

Christ ever continues the same loving, precious Lord. As we never lose our label as "sinners", so he never loses his name, nor changes his nature. His name is always *Jesus, the Saviour*: his nature is always *love*. Therefore put on Christ. Clothe your mind, memory and conscience afresh with the exceeding great and precious promises, which so freely flow from his lips. Hear his loving call, "Come unto me all you who are weary and heavy laden." Rejoice at his precious promise, "I will give you rest" (Matt. 11:28).

"Sweet Savior! what! Come to you, with all the burden of our sins, lusts and vile corruptions? Lord! how your thoughts are above our thoughts! O when we are sorely burdened with the weight of our sins and corruptions, we are ready to flee from you, and think you will have nothing to do with us—but will spurn us from your presence—if we presume to come to you. But, Lord, will you indeed refresh us, and give rest to us? Yes, it is high treason against you to suspect this! Lord, increase our faith. Pardon our unbelief. Lord, help us to believe you, and to cleave to you. For this your blessed word ever holds good—"According to your faith be it unto you" (Matt. 9:29).

Sixthly, it is the will of God the Holy Spirit that we should put on Christ. He at first convinced our minds of sin, made us sensible that we have no righteousness in ourselves, and caused our consciences to tremble under a sense of guilt. Why did he do this? Because he is the glorifier of Christ, and the comforter of all his beloved members. Therefore he would drive us out of our naked selves—to the fullness of Christ. He showed us the corrupt judgment we naturally have of ourselves, of sin, and of righteousness, that we might take shelter in nothing but the wounds of Jesus for our sins, clothe our minds with his righteousness, and that we should ever remember that all our salvation is in Christ, so that we might find in and from him, peace of conscience, joy of soul, and holiness of heart and life.

The Spirit still constantly bears witness to Christ, to the truth as it is in him, and takes of the things of Christ, and shows them to us. Why? Truly that we might receive, apply and appropriate them, so as to enjoy them in our mind, memory and conscience, for all the purposes of righteousness, peace and joy in the Holy Spirit. The Holy Spirit who gives us a new birth into Christ, breathes into us desires after Christ, and keeps those desires alive in our souls. All the exhortations in the word, to quicken us in looking to Christ, believing in Christ, and putting on, and cleaving to Christ, are given by his inspiration. Let us remember that it is through his gracious aid, that we ever do put on Christ. For the Spirit lovingly helps our infirmities. He enables us, from day to day, to look to Christ for salvation, to lean on Christ for strength, to put on Christ as our righteousness, to cleave to him as our Beloved, to enjoy fellowship with him, and to long for his coming, that we may be forever glorified with him!

But says Paul, "Now if any man have not the Spirit of Christ, he is not His" (Rom. 8:9). Therefore it is of the utmost importance to know, whether we have the Spirit of Christ. But how may we know this? If we see our want of Christ, and the worth of Christ, so as to desire him, to come unto him, to believe in him, and to put him on for pardon, peace, holiness and salvation, we have the Spirit of Christ. For without the Spirit we never could do this. Of ourselves, we have not the least sight, will, or inclination to this. But, if our hearts are inclined to this, we may be fully assured, it is from the Spirit's teaching and influence. — Therefore we may rest fully satisfied, that we have the Spirit of Christ. This is the address to Jehovah Jesus, of those who have his Spirit: "O Lord, we have waited for thee: the desire of our soul is to thy name, and to the remembrance of you" (Isa. 26:8). If such be the language of your heart — such the desire of your soul, O thou poor, doubting, distressed sinner, glory and rejoice, for you have the Spirit of Christ, as really as Paul had.

Thus the holy, blessed and glorious Trinity agree in one mind, to bear record of the *man* Christ Jesus to us, of our salvation in him. Therefore we should put him on continually, as the glory of our mind, the joy of our memory, and for the peace and comfort of our conscience. For it has pleased the Three-One-God, that all the promises, which are given to us, should be *in* Christ Jesus.

Seventhly, We should put on Christ; for "Unto us are given exceedingly great and precious promises, that by these we might be partakers of the divine nature" (2 Pet. 1:4). "Yes", says a poor sinner, — "but when I look at the precious promises of God, and look at myself, I see in me, so much vileness, so much unworthiness of any one promise, so much unfitness for it, and so much unsuitableness to the nature of it — that I stagger at the promise through unbelief, and never can think it belongs to me." True! There is not one promise, in all the book of God, that you are worthy of, or that belongs to you, considering *yourself*, as a sinner fallen from God. It would be the highest presumption in you, or the holiest man upon earth to think so.

But this is the glory of us poor sinners— "All the promises of God are in Christ Jesus, and in him they are yes and amen, (sure and certain to be fulfilled to us) unto the glory of God" (2 Cor. 1:20). Therefore if you do not put on Christ, you can enjoy no comfort from the sweet declarations and precious promises of God. Take, for instance, this blessed word: "The eyes of the Lord watch over the *righteous*, and his ears are open to their prayers" (1 Pet. 3:12). Now you see yourself to be a poor sinner—How then can you apply this to yourself, or take any comfort from it? You cannot, unless you put on Christ. For you are not righteous in yourself—but only in him; being clothed with his righteousness. Nor are the ears of God open to your prayers, only as you are accepted in his beloved Son, and as your prayers are presented in his name, and by him to the Father.

It is promised, "God will keep the feet of his saints" (1 Sam 2:9), that "precious in the sight of the Lord is the death of his saints" (Psa. 116:15), and that "Christ shall come to be glorified in his *saints*" (2 Thess. 1:10). Now you and I see ourselves sinners—How then can such precious declarations belong to us? We must ask—*who is a saint?* One who has received that mercy of God, bestowed on sinners, through Christ, in quickening and sanctifying them by his Holy Spirit. For as God loved us, chose us, and justifies us in Christ, so he also sanctifies and makes us holy in him. Hence we become the holy brethren of Christ, and are saints in him. So that all the precious promises being in him, are ours. For we are one with Christ.

"All things are ours;" all the promises of this life, as well as those of that which is to come; all are ours—because we are Christ's (1 Cor. 3:23). We are blessed, and shall be "blessed, with all spiritual, and all temporal blessings in Christ, by God the Father, according as he has chosen us in him" (Eph. 1:3). How sweet then to range through the sacred pages, and to take up one precious promise after another, and to claim them all as my own in Jesus, to the glory of God! Here is no presumption in this; nothing of the pride of the self-righteous Pharisee, who says, "this and the other promise belongs to me, because I am righteous, and holy, and good in myself."

But seeing the promises all in Christ, and putting on him, we enjoy the comfort of the promises, and rejoice in Christ, though we have no confidence in the flesh. Rejoice, because there is not one word of God, respecting this life, and our eternal state to come—but that which flows from the loving heart of a covenant God in, Christ. All shall be fulfilled, and made good to us, to the glory of the truth of the ever-blessed Promiser. O then let us put on Christ, and no more stagger at any of the promises, through unbelief. For our hope of eternal life is secure. God, who cannot lie, promised it in, and to Christ, before the world began (Titus 1:1).

Lastly, we should put on Christ, because he is appointed to be our judge. That very Jesus, who so loved us, as to expire in blood and anguish upon the accursed tree, a sacrifice for our sins—to judge our souls! What can bring such relief to our mind, such joy to our memory, such peace to our conscience—as this! O believer! how much below your privilege, do you live and act, if you are in continual dread and terror of soul, about the judgment day! True, it is most dreadful, it is most tremendous—to think of appearing before the Judge of the living and dead, to hear the solemn, the irreversible sentence of, "Come you blessed," or "Go you cursed."

But always remember who it is who will pronounce this solemn doom—it is your loving Savior, and gracious

Why We Should Put On Christ

justifier. It is that dear Christ, who bore our sins in his own body on the tree—who has put away our sins, by the sacrifice of himself—who has forever made an end of sins, made reconciliation for iniquity, and brought in an everlasting righteousness, perfectly and forever to justify us; so that this is the irreversible doom of justice itself, "There is now no condemnation to those who are in Christ Jesus." Nor will there be any condemnation brought against them, nor sentenced upon them, by their Judge in that solemn day. For they will be found in him divinely justified and forever acquitted from their sins. He knows well those whom he *redeemed*, by his own blood; he *justified* them in his own righteousness; he *sanctified* them by his own Spirit; and therefore, he will call to them, "Come you who are blessed, inherit my glory!"

Look back then to Christ on the cross by faith, and look forward to Christ on the judgment—seat with courage. Put on Christ, and put off your fears. Yes, put on Christ, and be filled with boldness, peace and joy, when you think on the judgment-day. For look, it is your loving and beloved bridegroom, who comes openly to espouse you to himself, in the presence of God, angels, and men; and this in consequence of your present personal espousal to him, by the Spirit, through faith. For have you chosen Chris as your only Savior? Do you flee to him as your only refuge? Do you cry to him to save you from your sins now, as well as from the wrath to come? Who gave you this heart and this faith? Truly, he who loved you, and died for you! And will he, can he—reject your soul, and sentence you, the object of his love, the purchase of his blood, the subject of his grace, the member of his body, of his flesh, and of his bones—to eternal wrath and destruction? Impossible! Dread to indulge the thought one moment. — For it is destructive of the joy of faith, and the workings of love.

"Behold, he shall come to be glorified and to be admired" (2 Thess. 1:10). O how will our Savior's glory shine forth, with the most resplendent luster, in his *loving, calling, justifying, sanctifying,* and *preserving* all his dear people unto eternal life! O how will he be admired in his saints, and by his saints — in his glorious *person,* in his precious offices, in his everlasting *love* to them, and in his everlasting *salvation* of them! Angels, archangels, and all the heavenly multitude, will then be struck with the greatest admiration, at beholding the full display of these things, which now they desire to look into. O you saints, what admiration, wonder and joy, will fill your enraptured souls — on seeing the glory which will then shine *in* you from your glorified head! "For when Christ, who is our life, shall appear, then shall we also appear." Where? At his left hand, with terror, shame and confusion? No! But we shall appear *with him in his glory* (Col. 3:4). And "so shall we be ever with the Lord." "Therefore. Comfort one another with these words" (1 Thess. 4:18).

Soul, from what do you seek comfort? Beware of your *feelings.* They often arise from a heated imagination, and lead to the worst kind of enthusiasm. I have known those, who have been engaged in pursuits, not at all becoming their profession, and yet have vainly talked of feeling the love of God. — Truly, if you find comfort in any other way, than what is agreeable to the holy words and sanctifying doctrines which testify of Christ, you will find yourself awfully deceived, and woefully disappointed in the end.

See then the proper work of faith, and the peculiar office of the Holy Spirit, and how they concur in comforting our souls. The Holy Spirit is a witness, as well as a comforter. He testifies of Jesus in the word: and he comforts the soul only by the belief of the word. Hence it is I have dwelt so largely on *why* we should put on the Christ, as revealed in the word. For, "By one offering he has perfected forever, those who are sanctified" (Heb. 10.14). That is, Christ made by the one sacrifice upon the cross of himself, once offered, a full, perfect, and sufficient satisfaction for sin. Nothing need—nothing can be added to it.

The work by which we are for ever perfected, is completely finished, and for ever done. He has perfectly fulfilled tho law for us; perfectly atoned to justice in our stead; perfectly expiated (paid for) our sins; obtained full pardon for and complete redemption from the curse of them; and perfectly justified us from all condemnation. Thus we are 'perfected forever.'

Who—us? Why, all who are sanctified—that is,

1. Separated and set apart by the choice of God the Father, from eternity—to partake of the perfect salvation of his beloved Son.

2. Sanctified, or separated by the Holy Spirit in time, from all our corrupt notions, self-righteous dependences, unholy ways, and sinful practices, to enjoy the perfect love, and salvation of the Son of God, by a holy faith. How simple is faith in its nature? It is neither more nor less than the 'belief of the truth.' How glorious is faith in its effects? It brings the fullness of the perfection of Christ's glorious work and salvation into the soul. Thus the very end of God's election is answered; for, "God hath from the beginning chosen us to salvation, through sanctification of the Spirit and belief of the truth"

(2 Thess. 2:13). Thus we are brought into a state of perfect peace with God. And while we put on Christ as our dear Friend, beloved Bridegroom, and precious Saviour, we shall rejoice, to think of his appearing as our Judge, to welcome us to the kingdom prepared for us, and which he has made us meet to enjoy.

> *If close to the Lord you would cleave,*
>   *Depend on his promise alone.*
> *His righteousness would you receive?*
>   *Then learn to renounce all your own.*
>
> *The faith of a Christian indeed,*
>   *Is more than mere notion or whim:*
> *United to Jesus our head,*
>   *We draw life and virtue from him.*
>
> *This God is the God we adore,*
>   *Our faithful unchangeable friend;*
> *Whose love is as large as his power,*
>   *And neither knows measure nor end.*
>
> *'Tis Jesus the first and the last,*
>   *Whose Spirit shall guide us safe home;*
> *We'll praise him for all that is past,*
>   *And trust him for all that's to come!*

Chapter 8

When We Should
Put On Christ

God's time is best. "And he says, "Behold, *now* is the accepted time; behold *now* is the day of salvation." Procrastination is *the thief of time*; and here it is *the murderer of comfort*. Behold, *now* you are called upon to put on Christ. Surely, it should be our boast and our glory, wherever we go, to carry Christ in our mind, memory, and conscience—in the image of his love, the record of his mercy, the miracle of his grace in converting us to himself, the miseries he endured for our sins, the sorrows he sustained for our salvation, the perfection of his atonement and righteousness, the victory of his cross, the triumphs of his resurrection, the prevalency of his intercession, the comfort and joy of his coming again to receive us to himself, that where he is, there we may eternally be. O if these things dwell constantly in us, we shall not only be alive—but lively in the work of faith, the labor of love, and the patience of hope; while we shall be dead to sin, and to all the pomps and vanities of a sinful world; and sweetly sing,

*"Wherever I turn, wherever I rove,
I meet the object of my love"*

I have read of a godly man who was once very dissolute. When converted, his former companions sought to bring him back to his former wicked courses. But he told them, "I am deeply engaged in meditating on a little book, which contains only three pages; so at present I have no time for other business."

Being asked again if he had finished his book, he replied, "No; for though it contains only three pages, yet there is so much comprised in them, that I have devoted myself to read therein, all the days of my life.

The first leaf is **red**. Here I mediate on the sufferings of my Lord and Savior, His shedding His precious blood, as an atonement for my sins, and a ransom for my soul, without which I must have been a damned sinner in hell, to all eternity!

The second leaf is **white**. This cheers my heart with the wonderful consideration of the unspeakable joys of heaven obtained for me by Christ--and of being forever with Him!

The third leaf is **black**. Here I think of the horrible state of the damned--and the perpetual torments they are suffering in hell. O this excites thankfulness to my Savior, for His wonderful love and rich grace, in snatching me as a brand out of the fire, and saving me from eternal destructions!"

Here is a good man, a good book, and a good example for you and me. "Let us go and do likewise." Constantly meditate upon Christ; upon the wrath He has saved us from--and the glory He has saved us for!

When We Should Put On Christ

Let us consider some peculiar times and seasons, in which more especially we should put on Christ.

First, When we approach *the throne of grace.* This, if we are alive to God, we shall do constantly. "Praying always," is the Christian's motto.

One can just as well conceive of a living man, entirely destitute of all fears, passions, hopes, affections, desires, of breath also, as of a regenerate soul, living without prayer to God. Prayer is the spiritual breathing of a quickened soul. At a throne of grace he pours out his hopes, fears, sorrows, affections and desires. But if his mind memory and conscience, is not clothed with Christ as his high priest, mediator and advocate before the throne of God above, he will find but little comfort, in drawing near to a throne of grace below. No, he will not draw near to God at all. Though he may find words, yet they will be without heart and hope. Prayer will be only a talk to satisfy conscience. It will be begun without confidence, performed without spirit, and ended without joy.

But if our minds are clothed with this comfortable truth, that we have a great high priest, who is passed into the heavens, Jesus the Son of God—then we shall see our heavenly Father seated on a throne of grace, with smiles of approbation and acceptance; and we shall come boldly to it, that we may obtain mercy as miserable sinners, and find grace to supply our wants as needy creatures. For it is only "through Jesus we have acceptance, by one Spirit, unto the Father" (Eph. 2:18). It is only "in Christ that we have boldness, and access with confidence by the faith of him" (Eph. 3:12). O believer, consider well these, your inestimable privileges. Here is *access*, which is a liberty to approach God as a Father. *Boldness*, which is a freedom of speech in delivering our whole heart and mind to God in prayer. *Confidence,* which is a well-grounded persuasion that our persons and performances shall find acceptance to God through Christ.

When a cause is to be tried its court, parties concerned are very busy. So is Satan in times of prayer. He acts as plaintiff and accuser. When he sees us on our knees, he will inject accusations into our minds, such as, "What! does such a vile sinner as you expect be heard by a holy God? Look back on your past conduct—no, think of what you did a little while ago—and look at yourself now—see what vain and wandering thoughts are in you —how cold, how dead, how distracted are all your prayers—can you think God will hear and accept you, and such prayers as yours?"

Satan is a mighty adversary to prayer. But put on Christ, and silence Satan. It is the joy of faith, that your audience and acceptance with God does not depend on what you are in yourself. But glory in this blessed truth, that to the praise of the glory of God's grace, your person is accepted in his beloved Son; and through his much incense your prayers shall be received and answered. O put on this blessed truth, and cast away every discouragement, "Having therefore, brethren, boldness to enter into the holiest by the blood of Jesus, by a new and living way which he has consecrated, through the veil; that is to say, his flesh; and having a high priest over the house of God, let us draw near with a true heart, in *full assurance of faith*" that our God will hear and accept us (Heb. 10:19). Joseph strictly commanded his brethren, if they would see his face with comfort—to bring his brother Benjamin with them. So if we expect any comfort from God's throne of grace, we must put on our dear Brother Christ, and carry him in the arms of our faith, and plead his worth and worthiness alone for access and acceptance.

Secondly, Put on Christ in your mind, memory and conscience, when you go to *his table*. If you live and walk as a believer in him, you cannot neglect this blessed institution of your dear Lord. If you do, all is not right between our Savior and your heart. By your neglect of this you rob your precious soul of a blessed privilege, of much comfort, and your dear Lord of his glory. But does a sight and sense of your unworthiness deter you? You cannot be humbled too low on account of this. If you were to live to the age of Methuselah, you would have no worth, nor worthiness in yourself, for which Christ should receive you. "Worthy is the Lamb." He is worthy of you, though you are not worthy of him. For he bought you with his blood, when you had done nothing to merit it, nor ever can do any thing to deserve it: therefore, clothe your mind with his precious love; your memory with his gracious promises; and your conscience with his glorious salvation. Go to his table to commemorate his dying love. Be constantly showing forth his death, as your only hope, till he comes. Be feeding on his flesh, and drinking his blood, till he receive you to himself. For he saith, "Whoso eats my flesh, and drinks my blood, has eternal life, and I will raise him up at the last day" (John 6:54). The more you feed on Christ, the more abundantly will you experience that you have eternal life in him; and the more joyful assurance will you have of being raised up by him. For he adds, "He who eats me, even he shall live by me" (John 6:57). Live a holy, happy, spiritual life—out of self—above nature—even a life of fellowship with Christ and his father, enjoying his peace and love, through the power of the Holy Spirit.

Thirdly, In seasons of *heaviness* — **put on Christ.** Peter describes believers as very joyful souls. "Wherein you greatly rejoice." Joy is a fruit of the Spirit. We are called upon to "rejoice in the Lord always; and again to rejoice." (Phil. 4:4). But in what do saints greatly rejoice? In their being the elect of God — sanctified by the Spirit — sprinkled by the blood of Christ — begotten to a lively hope — and kept by the power of God through faith unto salvation. O believer! these are never-failing springs of joy! But he adds, "though now for a season (if need be) you are in heaviness through manifold temptations" (1 Pet. 1:6): Has that season come? There is a need for it. Are you in heaviness through a sense of indwelling sin; pressed down under its weight, groaning under its burden, and distressed with manifold temptations? Why is all this permitted? He tells us, for the trial of our faith.

The Lord is testing your faith. Beware that you do not cast away your shield of faith, and see that you do not distrust Christ, by saying "he neither loves me, nor cares for me; but has cast me off forever." No — but rather call to mind his free grace in undertaking your cause, his great love in dying for your sins, his rich mercy in calling you to himself, and his faithfulness and truth which are pledged for your salvation. Remember that he is "anointed to give the garment of praise for the spirit of heaviness" (Isa. 61:3). Put him on; cleave to him; for the times of refreshing shall come from his presence. Christ is not only a friend while the warm sunshine of prosperity of soul lasts; but he is a friend who loves at all times, and a brother born for adversity. (Prov. 17:17).

Whatever we found him at the best,
He's at the worst the same.

Seasons of conflict, affliction, heaviness and temptation, are the best times for praying to the Lord; but the worst times for judging of our state. Jesus is not a 'summer bird'—who forsakes his people in the winter of adversity. No! He ever lives to save them to the very uttermost. Heaviness is not to destroy your confidence—but only to test your faith. See what the blessed end of it shall be. Your faith is much more precious than gold. Therefore not a grain shall be lost in the fire. But it shall be found unto praise and honor and glory at the appearing of Jesus Christ. O let your mind, memory and conscience be clothed with this precious truth. "His anger endures but for a moment. In his favor is life; heaviness may endure for a night—but joy comes in the morning" (Psa. 30:5).

Fourthly, In a season of *darkness* and desertion of soul, put on Christ, who is the light of life. It is a sure mark of a regenerate soul, and a loving heart, that it is troubled, and mourns for its darkness, when the Lord hides his face. And it is the proper work of a renewed mind, to apply to Christ—a sanctified memory to retain Christ—and of a good conscience not to rest satisfied without Christ. "Truly you are a God who hides yourself, O God of Israel, the Savior" (Isa. 49:15). But why does God hide his face, and leave any of his dear children to mourn in darkness? That is your proper work to look to, and inquire for yourself. Let the cause be what it may, the purpose is not to drive you from your God, nor to make you let go of your confidence in Christ. No; but quite the contrary; to make you the more to trust in him, and to stay your soul upon him. He is the God of Israel, and the Savior, though he hides his face. Examine your soul. Search your ways. See if some cursed lust, or Christ-dishonoring pride, some pleasure in sin, or vain confidence in yourself and your own righteousness, has not caused your Lord to hide away his face. Therefore, humble yourselves under the mighty hand of God. Be afflicted, and mourn and weep. Pour out your heart to the Lord. Confess your sin to him, and be ashamed of your folly before him. Tell him,

> *I cannot live without your light*
> *Cast out and banished from your sight.*

Cicero, when banished from Italy, and Demosthenes, when banished from Athens, wept every time they looked towards their own country. Poor deserted believer, dost not thou mourn every time you look to your heavenly country? Do not tears trickle down your cheeks, when you think of your God. and canst not see the smiles of bis face as heretofore? O, this mourning of his absence is a sure sign of the presence of love to him, and longing for him.

Therefore, beware, while you loathe yourself, and bemoan your folly, that you do not dishonor your Lord by suspecting his everlasting love, questioning his precious truths, or neglecting his glorious salvation. Now, even now, put on your precious Christ afresh; mind and remember his sweet declaration to his Father, concerning all his people: "You have loved them, as you have loved me" (John 17:23); even with the very same everlasting unchangeable love. Therefore, though in darkness and sorrow, be assured, God's love is always the same, like himself, without variableness. Though he hides his face, still he rests in his love. For, God did not love you, choose you and call you, for any good he saw in you—but he loved you, and viewed you in Christ. And in Christ he is ever the same covenant God, and reconciled Father, whether he consoles with his love, or chastises with his rod; whether he lifts up the light of his countenance upon

When We Should Put On Christ

you, or hides away his face from you. Your sin and folly may cause him to change his conduct towards you—but he can never, never change his covenant, name and nature, For *God is love* (1 John 4:16).

God loves you in Christ, views you in him, has accepted, pardoned, justified and sanctified you in Christ. Be ever looking to Christ, clothing your mind with him, remembering his loving kindness, and pleading in your conscience his atonement for your sins, his righteousness as your justification, and the salvation he has finished for your soul. Though at present you see not the light of comfort, nor feel the sunshine of joy, yet glory in the word of truth and grace as it is in Jesus. This ever abides with you, though comfort forsakes you. Search the scriptures. Study them. Pray over them. They testify of Christ; of the covenant of grace made with him ; of a covenant God in him ; and of all the covenant blessings promised to us poor sinners by him. Listen to that sweet voice of love which salutes your ears, and gives counsel to your soul. Are you mourning in darkness, and complaining in sadness, "My Lord hath forsaken me, my God hath forgotten me?" Hear the Lord's answer, "Can a woman forget her nursing child, that she should not have compassion on the son of her womb? Yea, they may forget, yet will I never forget you" (Isa. 49:13).

Though your God and Father hides his face, yet he hath not forgotten you. He lovingly enquires after you, and sweetly gives advice in the following words; "Who is among you that fears the Lord; that obeys the voice of his servant; that walks in darkness, and has no light?" (Isa. 50:10). Your character is here described, as plainly as though your very name was written in full length.—You walk in darkness, under the hidings of God's face. You see not the light of God's countenance shining upon your soul. You are without spiritual joy and comfort of heart. This is your distress. Still, you fear the Lord. Therefore your jealous concern about the cause of your darkness; your sorrow for it; and your prayers and desires to be delivered from it. You obey Christ, who, as man, is the servant of God, by believing in him as the only Savior, and expecting salvation from him *alone*.

Now, what is the counsel the Lord gives you? What is his will concerning you? He has put you into the school of darkness, to learn to hear his voice, and obey his will, to exercise your graces upon him, and thereby to honor him. Peter, when on the Mount, was for building tabernacles for residence: but he must be brought low. So the Lord brings you low from the mount of joy, into the dark valley, that you should make him your only trust and stay, and your dwelling-place. Therefore, Hear and obey his sweet counsel. "Let him trust in the name of the Lord, and rely upon his God." Here is *trusting* opposed to *seeing*. "The name of the Lord is a strong tower, the righteous runs into it, and is safe" (Prov. 18:10). This text has puzzled me. For what has the man who is righteous in himself, to fear? Why should he want a tower of defense? Why should he run into it for safety? Surely, if he is righteous in himself, he need not flee from himself; he can take refuge in his own righteousness; he is safe in himself. But this is the sentence of the God of truth, "There is none righteous, no, not one" (Rom. 3:10). Then, that man who dares trust in himself, is arraigned and condemned by our Lord as a Pharisee; he displays the ignorance and pride of his heart, and in effect, arrogantly says to Christ, "I have no need to flee unto thee as a refuge, nor to trust in thy righteousness to justify me." Therefore this text can only be understood of the poor, convinced, humble sinner, who sees his own righteousness as filthy rags, quits all confidence in it, flies from it, and runs to take shelter in the name of the Lord; even that blessed name, Jesus, which is above every other name. To him his knee bows, his humbled heart submits, arid his enlightened soul trusts and glories alone in that name, whereby Jesus is called, "The Lord our righteousness" (Jer. 23:6). Such, and only such a one, is a righteous person in the sight of God.

Now you are called to *trust* in this name of the Lord. This is opposed to all other means and props whatever; to all comfortable sense of God's love; to all sight of grace, any righteousness, any hope, you have in yourself. It is to put on Christ afresh as the Lord your righteousness, strength and salvation; to clothe your mind, memory and conscience, with Christ your only confidence, in the darkest seasons, and most distressing moments, even when all other trust and confidence forsake you. Now honor your God by the claim of your faith. With the church of old cry out in confidence, "Behold, God is my salvation; I will trust, and will not be afraid; for the Lord God is my strength and my song; and he has become my salvation" (Isa. 12:2).

Perhaps, you are now writing bitter things against yourself. You are thinking, 'All is dark and disconsolate within; I cannot see that I have a single grace to stay my soul upon. It is not only dark, but tempestuous also. One wave of corruption rolls over another. The storms of justice are over my head. I fear vengeance is pursuing me. Black clouds of unbelief hang heavy on me, while the enemy suggests within me, Where is now thy God? Alas, what will become of me? What must I, what shall I do, in the hour, and power of darkness?'

Behold, here is a cordial held forth to revive your drooping mind, and to support your sinking spirits. Hear and obey the voice of your *Wonderful Counsellor*; "Let him *stay* himself upon his God." His God still, though he walks in darkness, and has no light. God in Christ is still your God. Stay your soul upon this. Are you weak, weary, faint, and ready to fall? Then lean upon your God for support and strength. Clothe your mind, memory and conscience with Christ: with God manifested in him, reconciled to you, at peace with you: your covenant God and Father in Christ; and with all the exceeding great and precious promises, which he hath given us in him; and take up the sweet claim of faith, and cry in the importunate prayer of your dear Lord, "*My* God, *my* God, why have you forsaken me?" Thus trust and stay, believe and hope, cleave and lean, call upon and pray to the Lord *your* God, O you children of light, while you walk in darkness! For, so he lovingly commands you.

O the happy privilege! The precious counsel! The cheering comfort! The supporting strength! contained in these words of the Lord, by Isaiah, to all his dear children, who walk in darkness, and see no light! Spirit of all grace, help us to obey this precious word, to put on Christ who is the light of life, to trust in him, and to stay our souls upon him, whenever we walk in darkness, and see no light. O soul! let not this truth forsake thee; bind it about thy neck; write it upon the table of thine heart; it shall be health to thy navel, and marrow to thy bones — *our safety and security entirely depend on the love of God's heart to us, and the hold his omnipotent arm of grace has of us; while our comfort arises from our laying hold of Christ, cleaving close to him, and abiding steadfastly in him.* 'Hence,' says St. Paul, 'I am apprehended,' or caught hold of by Christ Jesus. What then? Why, says he, I strive, by all means, to '

When We Should Put On Christ

apprehend,¹ take fast hold on, and to have full possession of this precious Christ, who first apprehended me (Phil. 3:12). This is the genuine work of faith—this the labor of every Christian— this the experience of every sinner apprehended by Christ.

When that great emperor Julius Caesar was at any time sad and dejected in his mind, he used to say to himself, "Remember, that you are Caesar!" This thought revived his spirits. Thus, O soul, in your darkest seasons and heaviest state, "remember that you are a Christian; Jesus is your Savior; God is your Father; the Holy Spirit is your Comforter!" Stay thy mind upon this; plead and wait for the comfort of this. "Therefore will the Lord wait, that he may be gracious unto you; and therefore will he be exalted, that he may have mercy upon you: for the Lord is a God of judgment; blessed are all they who wait for him" (Isa. 30:18).

Fifthly, When in *worldly trials*, and bodily afflictions,—put on Christ. These are our dear Lord's *precious legacies* to all his beloved followers. Just before he left the world, he told us, "In the world you shall have trouble." But this will be very hard to endure, if we do not have Christ with us, in our trials and afflictions. But mind how tribulation is placed. It stands between peace and victory. Peace is in the front; victory brings up the rear. Blessed be his love: thus our dear Lord begins, "These things have I spoken unto you, that *in me* you might have peace. In the world you shall have tribulation." Blessed be his power: thus he ends, "But be of good cheer, I have overcome the world" (John 16:33). Just as though he had said, In the midst of your tribulations, let them be of whatever kind, clothe your mind and memory with those things which I have spoken unto you, that you may have peace of conscience. Remember the peace I have made for you, by my blood on the cross. I am your peace. In *me* you shall find peace. Let none of your tribulations distress your conscience. For none of them shall destroy your souls; for I have overcome the world, and all the evils of it. My conquests are your victories. Therefore be of good cheer.

When we believe this; when we put on Christ, and his precious words, we find and feel consolation in the midst of tribulation; "for this is the victory that overcomes the world, even our faith" (1 John 5:4). But how does faith overcome the world, and all the tribulations we meet with in it? By bringing Christ, his victories and his strength, into the heart, and by presenting to the mind the prospect of heaven and glory. Then the world loses its hold of the heart, it sinks in the soul's esteem, and is brought under the feet. And as to its tribulations, upon a just estimate, the believer says, "I reckon that the sufferings of this present time are not worthy to be compared with the glory which shall be revealed in us" (Rom. 8:18) O precious Jesus! how inexpressibly precious is your presence to the soul, when in the furnace of affliction!

Pliny mentions certain trees which grow in the Red Sea, which, though beaten upon by the waves—they stand like an immovable rock. Yet, in full sea, they are quite covered with water. Yet it appears by many proofs, that they are bettered by the roughness of the sea. Just so, a Christian planted in the Red Sea of Christ's blood, is armored against all the waves of temptation; and is improved by afflictions. The more he is beat upon, though overwhelmed with the billows of distress and trouble— the better he thrives, and the more his soul flourishes in spiritual grace! For this is the loving design of our Lord

When We Should Put On Christ

in all our troubles and afflictions—to wean us from the world, and to endear himself to us! So that every affliction has its commission from him. It comes with the impress of his love. Its contents runs thus: "Your Lord sees that through too much ease and prosperity in this world, you are prone to forget him; therefore he calls on you by this, to put him on more ardently, that you may enjoy him and his love more comfortably, in your mind, memory, and conscience." See to it then. Look up to him, that this blessed end be answered.

I have often found by experience, and confessed with joy, that a sick bed has proved like a hotbed to my soul. It has drawn up warm desires, and longing affections to Christ. And I have sweetly found the Sun of Righteousness arising upon me, reviving, cheering and comforting my soul. It is only Christ put on in the mind, memory and conscience, that can support under trials, yield patience and comfort in afflictions, and sanctify all of them to the soul's profit. When afflictions are most heavy, Christ's presence makes the world and its troubles most light.

It is your wisdom to see then rod of chastisement in the hand of your loving heavenly Father. But God is a Father to us only in Christ. We are his children by faith in Christ (Gal. 3:26). Therefore, we can only see, know, and rejoice in him, and submit to him as our Father, by putting on Christ our elder Brother. Take Jesus with you in all your sufferings, and you shall find that as sufferings abound in you, consolations from him shall also abound to you from him.

It is your glory to see that all your afflictions are chastenings from the Lord; that they are all in love; that in all, he deals with you as with a son in whom he delights, and whom he designs to profit. He does not punish you with vindictive wrath—he is not taking vengeance of you for your sins. But how can you see this, except you put on Christ, in whom God had received full satisfaction for all your sins; has freely forgiven you all for Christ's sake; and has fully justified you from all in him? So that, strictly speaking, God, your Father, is not so much punishing you *for* your sins, as *from* your sins. That is, in all his chastisements he intends your spiritual good, that you should be more and more a partaker of Christ and his holiness; that sin may be more exceedingly sinful; yourself more vile in your own eyes, and more humbled before him, and your Savior more inestimably precious to your soul. So that all affliction, is a rod of love to whip you from the world, self and sin--into Christ, that you should put him on, and enjoy Him, who is your righteousness, life and salvation.

Then in and under all, so put on Christ that you may say with Job, "Though he slays me, yet will I trust in him" (Job 13:15). For I know him; I know that he is my Redeemer; that he ever lives to pray for me, to support me, and to save me to the very uttermost. If Christ is with us in all, all will be well with us. Could Caesar say to the trembling mariner, in a violent storm, "Be not afraid, for you carry Caesar?" O well may you say to your soul, in every storm of affliction, be not afraid, for you carry Jesus the Savior! He says, "Fear not, for I have redeemed you; I have called you by your name; you are mine. When you pass through the waters I will be with you; and through the rivers they shall not overflow you. When you walk through the fire you shall not be burnt; neither shall the flame kindle upon you." Now, why all this safety, in times of fiercest troubles and greatest dangers? Hear and rejoice. You are the claim of Jesus. He has

When We Should Put On Christ

redeemed, and called you. He challenges you as his own purchase, bought with the price of his precious blood. And that you may claim him; he says, "For I am the Lord *your* God, the Holy One of Israel, *your Saviour*" (Isa. 43:2, 3). Then, in all your troubles, put on Christ; clothe your mind, memory and conscience with all that is contained in that precious, soul-comforting word, *your Saviour*.

Luther used to say, "Come what will, in spite of the devil and all his children, we will sing the forty-sixth Psalm." O 'tis a most precious triumphant one! It begins with the joyful confidence of faith, "God is our refuge and strength, a very present help in trouble." It is replete with consolation; and it ends with the triumph of experience. "The Lord of hosts is with us; the God of Jacob is our refuge." Consider this; dwell on this; glory in this.

Sixthly, As we are to put on Christ in our heaviest and worst state, so we are also to put him on in our best and *most lively* state. — And this for one and the very same reason, because we are commanded to glory of him *only*, and to rejoice in him *always*. But we are prone to be elated with pride at our good fortune, and dejected to distress at our bad ones. For, when we find ourselves in a good fortunes, we think we have then put on Christ. This is much to be doubted; yea, it is greatly to be suspected, that we too often let go Christ, and cleave to our good fortune, and fine feelings.

What do you think of *Peter?* Was he not in a fine disposition and comfortable feeling, when he so boldly declared to his Lord, "Though all others should deny you, yet will I never deny you! I am ready to go with you into prison, and to death!" Can we doubt but that he was clothed with self-confidence, instead of putting on Christ his strength, and crying to him, as he did in his sinking disposition, "Lord save me—or I perish!" But after Satan had sifted Peter, we hear him no more boasting of his zeal for his Lord. It was then, "Lord, *you know* whether I love you, and how much I love you." He had now done with talking about his great love, and his perfect love to Christ—and was more taken up with the great and perfect love of Christ to him.

Paul was in danger of being exalted above measure, through the abundance of revelations which were given him. As Satan sifted Peter, so he buffeted Paul. This drove him to his right place, the feet of Christ; to his proper station, the throne of grace; to obtain mercy, and find grace to help in his time of need; to clothe his mind with the right object, Christ, and to cause his heart to trust in, and depend alone upon the grace of Christ, and not to be exalted at what he had been favored with, and with what he found and felt in himself.

Thus the church of old is charged by the Lord; "You trusted in your own beauty—and played the harlot because of your renown." Now, how did she come by her beauty, and to be renowned for her beauty? "It was perfect, through the loveliness which I had put upon you—says the Lord God" (Ezek. 16:14, 15).

What a monster of pride is man! How full of that cursed venom is human nature! We cannot receive any grace or blessing from the Lord—but corrupt nature is prone to be proud of it, to trust in it, and to boast in it. No one is exempt from this. I appeal to your hearts. I refer to your experience. When your heart has been enlarged in prayer; carried out in humblings, meltings, longings, aspirings, etc.—when you have heard the Word with warm affections and heavenly joy—; have communicated with a rapture of love; when your tongue has talked of Christ to others with sweetness and liberty; when your hand has been stretched forth to do any good work; in all these, have you not found pride very busy? Have not you been ready to pat yourself on your own back with pleasure, and to reflect with delight: "Well, now I am somebody indeed; now the Lord loves me truly; surely he loves me better, now I find myself so sweet, and feel myself so comfortable?" If you have not found it so, I know one who has.—But shame on us for this! God be merciful to us! For where is our precious Christ all this while? Not put on in our mind, memory and conscience. No. But we have looked at ourselves, till we have fallen in love with ourselves, and lost sight of him. We have been admiring our vile selves for our graces, instead of being in raptures with Jesus, who is altogether lovely, in whom all fullness dwells, and of whose fullness we receive grace for grace! To beat down pride, and sink into the depth of humility, Paul demands, "Who makes you to differ from another? and what do you have that you did not receive? Now, if you did receive it, why do you glory, as if you had not received it?" (1 Cor. 4: 7). *Thus* intimating, that we should turn our eyes from the gift, to the giver—from ourselves to our Lord. And whatever difference there is in us from another, we should account it all to the sovereign will of God. By his distinguishing grace God makes one man to differ from another, by freely bestowing favor on whom he wills, which he owes to no one. This is hard work to proud hearts. We forget that we stand by faith, and so become high-minded; we get into a high opinion of ourselves—what we are in ourselves, and what we can do for ourselves, and towards our own salvation.

This is the spirit the Galatian church fell into, which prevails much in this day. Hence our full and final justification by Christ is opposed, and our justification at the last day is insisted on to be by our works, by what is found in us, or done by us.

But this unscriptural notion exalts the creature, and debases the Saviour: supplants the work of Christ's obedience, to establish our own works and righteousness. *Our own righteousness sticks as close to us as our sins.* A secret confidence in it, is the strong citadel and chief fort, wherein the great strength of our enmity against Christ and his righteousness lies. Hence, in the act of faith, we find the motions of spiritual pride ever starting up. But you never can, or will get rid of the character of a sinner: therefore lie low; and see your need of the perfect righteousness of your Surety.

Put on Christ in opposition to all proud notions. Come out, and be separate from such principles, and the Lord will receive you. God views you, loves you, pardons you, justifies you, accepts you, delights in you, rejoices over you, and blesses you, with all spiritual blessings in *Christ*, according as he has chosen you in him, before the foundation of the world. This is the faith you are to live and walk by. Therefore be not high-minded, but fear. Fear the pride of self-righteousness. If you do not live and walk by the faith of this, you grieve the Spirit, the witness for Jesus, and lose your sweet, elevated, joyful estate. For, if in any sense we trust in and value ourselves upon them, they rival the Saviour, and counteract our faith. When we lose sight of Christ, our comfortable disposition is gone, and our minds sink into dejection and distress.

Should we keep our good dispositions? Let us look *through* them to Christ, *in* and *from* whom we receive them. While we feel ourselves happy, let us put on Christ in our mind and memory, who obtained peace for us by his blood, and believing in whom, we are filled with joy and peace through the power of the Holy Spirit. Therefore, be clothed with humility. The Psalmist, feeling some thought of pride like a buzzing fly, alighting upon his soul, beats it away with, "Not unto us, O Lord." It alights a second time; he slaps it away with, "Not unto us!" It comes a third time, and he thus kills it dead—"But unto your name give glory, for your mercy, and for your truth's sake" (Psa. 115:1). O How does the sight of mercy and truth make pride flee, and humility abound!

Seventhly, In the view of *death*, put on Christ. Well, Christian! All hail! I congratulate you. You have but one step more to take, before you will be at home with your Lord. Then you shall forever put on your Jesus in glory, and immortality. For truly, there is but a step between you and death. Soon, very soon you must put your foot into Jordan's cold stream, and must pass through the river death, to your promised inheritance. Do you shudder at the thought? Why should you? For,

> *"Faith builds a bridge across the gulf of death.*
> *Death's terror, is the mountain faith removes.*
> *'Tis faith disarms destruction; and absolves,*
> *From every clamorous charge, the guiltless tomb."*

Faith of itself, is but as an empty hand. How then can faith effect all this? O it brings its author and object *Jesus* —into the heart. By putting on Christ; by clothing the mind, memory, and conscience with the victories of Christ; we become triumphant conquerors over death and the grace. Thus faith does all, through Jesus, who is all in all. Long before our Almighty Conqueror took on flesh, with dauntless resolution he says, "O death, I will be your plague! O grave, I will be your destruction!"

(Hos. 13:14). He has fulfilled his word to the uttermost. "He has abolished death" (2 Tim. 1:10). He has annulled, destroyed and repealed it. As to all his redeemed, death it is not a penal evil, for Christ has taken away its sting, removed its curse, and changed it into the precious blessing of *sleep*. They only "sleep in Jesus." — "sleep in Jesus" (1 Thess. 4:14). Believe this. Put off your fears of death, and joyfully sing, "O death, where is your sting!" It is taken out by Christ. "O grave, where is your victory?" You are conquered by my Christ. Thanks, eternal thanks, be to God, who gives us the victory, through our Lord Jesus Christ. Faith receives the victory, puts it on, and wears it. Faith disarms destruction, it silences every clamorous charge of sin, and it makes even the dreary tomb, guiltless, and glorious.

But, if death is conquered, yet you dread *dying*; for you say, death has not lost its power to hurt you. Yes — but it has! For Jesus has destroyed him who "had the power of death; that is the devil." So that death is not only conquered — but the power of death and the devil is destroyed. How did Christ effect this? Why, "the sting of death is sin." This, he bore in his own body on the tree! This, he washed away by his own body upon the cross! This, he has forever taken away, and justified us from, by his resurrection from the dead. So that divine justice itself says, "Deliver the sinner, for I have found a ransom!" (Job 33:24). "The strength of sin is the law." The strength of every curse of the law — Christ has fully sustained and suffered. The strength of every command of the law — Jesus perfectly obeyed and fulfilled. Thus death is disarmed both of his strength and sting. Then put on Christ's atonement for your sins, and Christ's obedience unto death, for your justification, in your mind, memory and conscience, so you will have living comforts in dying hours; your heart will rejoice in Jesus; and you will sing victory in death.

If Jesus is with you, you will say with David, "Though I walk through the valley of the shadow of death, I will fear no evil." And with Paul, you will take up this triumphant challenge, "Who shall separate me from the love of Christ?" (Rom. 8:35). "Shall death?" No! For says he, "Death is yours!" (1 Cor. 3:22) Your conquered enemy cannot hurt you. Your covenant friend in Christ, it is commissioned to summon you from a world of vanity and woe, and a body of sin and death, to the blissful regions of glory and immortality, to meet your Lord, and be for ever with him. "

When the perishable has been clothed with the imperishable, and the mortal with immortality, then the saying that is written will come true– Death has been swallowed up in victory!" – 1 Corinthians 15:54

In the Marian persecution, a godly woman was brought before bloody Bonner, bishop of London, on account of her faith in Christ. The bishop threatened he would take her husband from her. She said, "Christ is my husband!" He said, "I will take away your child." She replied, "Christ is better to me than ten sons!" He said, "I will strip you of all your comforts!" She said, "Christ is mine, and you cannot strip me of Him! Take away what you will, you cannot take away my Christ from me!" So death may threaten to take all from you, but you may boldly put death at defiance, as she did Satan's bishop. Having Christ in your mind, memory and conscience, you will take a smiling leave of the world, and say, "Sovereign Lord, as you have promised, you now dismiss your servant in peace, for my eyes have seen your salvation!" (Luke 2:29, 30).

Christ the pearl of great price

What a pearl of glory lies,
 Hid in the gospel field!
What a jewel of great price,
 Is in the word revealed!

Who can set its virtues forth,
 How exquisite its glories are!
Its inestimable worth,
 What mortal can declare?

When this goodly pearl I wear,
 And put this jewel on,
I shall covet nothing here,
 But tread these trifles down:

Then my heart will be above;
 My joy and treasure will be there.
I shall walk in light and love,
 And with my Lord appear.

Chapter 9

Happy Consequences
of Thus Putting On Christ

When Alexander set out on his great exploit of conquering the world, before he left Macedonia, he divided among his captains and friends all that he had. For which one of his friends reproved him, for being so profuse as to reserve nothing for himself. Alexander replied, "I have reserved much for myself; for I am full of hope, of being the monarch of the whole world, which, by the help of my captains and nobles, I expect to gain." Was he content to set out with nothing, but the possession of this hope? O Christian, what is this hope compared to yours? A hope full of immortality! Though with Alexander you part with all things, yet putting on Christ you possess all in him. O the infinite blessedness of this, "Christ in you the hope of glory!" Though you do not hope to be the monarch of the world, yet you have that faith which "overcomes the world," and have infinitely greater honor, in being an heir of God, and a joint heir with Christ. For this world, and all things in it, shall be burnt up; but you shall live and reign with Christ to all eternity. Most glorious effects of putting on Christ! Yea, before we arrive at the heavenly mansions, we shall experience the happy consequences of putting on Christ.

1. We shall not only be alive to God, but *lively in our souls*, and *lively in his service*. We shall not be sluggish, and crawl heavily in the ways of God; but shall walk with pleasure, yea, run with delight, the way of his commandments. For, we shall find this promise fulfilled, "They shall renew their strength; mount up with wings as eagles; run, and not be weary; walk, and not faint" (Isa. 40:31). Whatever we do, we shall do it heartily, as unto the Lord. We shall ardently strive against sin, resolutely resist Satan, and sweetly go on, 'perfecting holiness in the fear of God.' Thus we shall honor the gospel; adorn its doctrines; manifest the glory of grace; and glorify the God of our salvation: while at the same time we shall reprove, if not improve, that race of dull, formal, sleepy professors, who have neither life nor spirit in the ways of God. Though in the visible church, they have a name to live, yet they appear to be as dead, to any life of communion with Christ, liveliness of spirit from him, and cheerful devotedness of heart, lip and life to his glory,as the carnally dead in sin. What the poet says in a natural sense, may justly be applied to such in a spiritual one:

> *"He soundly slept the night away,*
> *And just did— nothing all the day."*

It is a recommendation of that useful animal, a horse, that he is 'sound wind and limb.' It cannot be said so of many professors. For though their wind may be sound enough, to talk of the doctrines of the gospel, yet they are not sound in limb: they halt and tire in the ways of God, instead of running the heavenly race. Though they are all life and activity to carnal things; yet, they are cold and

Happy Consequences of thus Putting On Christ

lifeless to spiritual things. Such must stand reproved, by the spiritual liveliness of warm-hearted Christians, and the evidence which they give of their inward enjoyment of Christ's love ; rich experience of his presence and power ; that they are feeding upon him in their hearts, and growing up into him in all things, who is the chief object of their affections, and the one absorbing desire of their souls.

O how little of this is to be found among professors! More, to insist too much on this, will sometimes draw forth, from a sleeping professor, an evidence that he is not quite dead. For, he will just open his eyes, look upon you with contempt, and yawn out, "Ah, this is *mere enthusiasm*—a young thing on the mount, in its first love." So that it really seems by such, that it is to the honor of old Christians, that they have left their first love. Ah—but it is poor profession, without true affections. They are sorry professors--whose heads are furnished only with cold notions--while their hearts are destitute of warm love. What shall we say of such? That they are really in Christ, and put him on? It is to be questioned. Yes, they question it themselves. Are they truly alive to Christ? It is to be doubted. Yes, they doubt it themselves. They live in dreadful suspense. At times, when conscience is a little roused, they complain of doubts, and express their fears, whether they have an interest in Christ or not. Is this at all to be wondered at? For, instead of putting on Christ, and not making provision for the flesh to fulfill the lusts thereof; they put *off* Christ, *disobey* his commands, live after the *flesh*, and walk according to the course of this present evil world.

See then the blessed effect of putting on Christ, in having your spirit lively, your affections warm, your disposition comfortable, and your soul ardently pressing, 'towards the mark for the prize of your high calling of God in Christ Jesus.'

2. You will *receive the witness of the Spirit*, and live in the joyful experience of this truth—"God is Love." He will shed his love abroad in your heart by the Holy Spirit. The peace of God which passes all understanding shall keep your heart and mind through Jesus Christ; and the Spirit himself will bear witness with your spirit that you are a child of God. For, says our dear Lord, "If a man loves me he will keep my words, and my Father will love him, and we will come unto him, and make our abode with him" (John 14:23). What a blessed word is this! What a wonderful mystery does it hold forth to us! What a full proof of the trinity of persons in the Godhead, the covenant love, and condescending grace of the triune God, Father, Son and Holy Spirit. Not only in coming to —but *dwelling in*, and taking up their abode in the hearts of poor sinners. O marvelous mystery of love. The persons who are thus honored, are all those "who love Christ and keep his words." That is, those who put him on, believing the word of his grace, and live under the influence of the doctrines he taught, the precepts he gave, and the ordinances he appointed.

But now, is not the Spirit's witness of the Father's love to us, and of our interest in Christ's salvation, the common privilege of all believers? Doubtless it is. Yet, without breach of love, it may be asserted, the most professors rest short of it. Some are quite easy and contented without it. Others, for lack of it, are at times, in perplexing doubts, dejecting fears, and dreadful uncertainties, whether they are the children of God. Or that they have redemption in the blood of Christ, even the forgiveness of their sins, or not. But, why is it thus? It cannot be for lack of encouragement from the word of our Lord. For thus runs his most generous charter, "If you abide in me, and my words abide in you, you shall ask what you will, and it shall be done unto you" (John 15:7). Again, "Ask and you shall receive, that your joy may be full" John 16:24). Fathers, "If you being evil, know how to give good gifts to your children, *how much more* shall your heavenly Father give his Holy Spirit to those who ask him?" (Luke 11:13).

That our Lord here speaks of the Spirit of adoption, in filling their souls with fullness of joy, by bearing witness with their spirits that they are children of God, cannot be doubted. That without his assurance, their joy cannot be full, must be granted. And that he here means to stir up and urge *all* his disciples to ask and plead for this most comfortable blessing, cannot be denied. Why then is not this inestimable privilege, which is common to all believers, enjoyed? Our Lord very plainly suggests the reason. There is a condition expressed, upon which the blessing is suspended. This condition not being complied with—the comfort is not enjoyed. Mind how our Lord's words run: "IF you abide in me and my words abide in you, you shall ask what you will, and it shall be done to you". Though salvation is absolutely sure, and infallibly certain to every believer, by the immutable decree of God, through the redemption of Christ; yet the comfortable knowledge and assurance of our own interest in it, can only be enjoyed by abiding in Christ: or as our Lord himself explains it, "IF my words abide in you." That is, "if the doctrines of my grace and love, and the truths of my salvation, are rooted in your mind, fixed in your memory, and established in your conscience—so as that you are living and feeding upon them holding fast the steady profession of them, steadfastly abiding by them, and living under the influence of them—then ask what you will, and it shall be done to you. Your Father will give his Holy Spirit to you, to bear witness with your spirit, that you are his children—thus your joy shall be full—you shall be filled with all joy and peace in believing."

Hence, it is most plain, that assurance by the witness of the Spirit, can only be enjoyed by putting on Christ, and steadfastly cleaving to him in heart, hope and affection. For lack of this, many go on heavily, without the witness of the Spirit. They do not put on the Lord Jesus in the whole affection of their soul. They do not fully honor him by the faith of their hearts. They do not keep his words, nor abide in him, clothe their minds with his precious truths, nor record his wonderful love in their memory, nor live enough upon his finished salvation in their conscience, and so are not wholly given up to Christ's glory, in their lives and conversations. But, spiritual sloth, worldly-mindedness, and carnality of affections so prevail, that they do not give all diligence to make their election sure—do not attend to that solemn prohibition, "Love not the world, neither the things that are in the world"—do not regard that awful assertion, "If any man love the world, the love of the Father is not in him" (1 John 2:15).

This will ever be found true in experience, even if the heart is given up to the world, it will sometimes appear to lose the sense of God's love. Some cursed thing exists, which rivals Christ in the heart, and grieves the Holy Spirit: therefore he withholds his comforting witness from their spirits. Hence the edge of prayer is blunted: they have not boldness at the throne of grace to ask with power, plead with importunity, and wrestle with vehemence, like Jacob, saying, "I will not let you go—unless you bless me."

See then the unspeakable blessedness of putting on Christ, in the happy enjoyment of the Spirit's witness. For, hereby you will be able to say, "My beloved is mine, and I am his" (Song. 2:16), and "Christ loved me, and gave himself for me" (Gal. 2:20). Thus you will enjoy, not only the reviving consolation of the safety of your present state; but also of your certain perseverance unto eternal glory. You will not merely take up with the notion —*once in grace, and always in grace*—but you will live in the comfort of this Christ-endearing truth, "Having loved his own, he loved them to the end" (John 13:1).

3. By putting on Christ, you will *put off the love of this world;* you will live above the world, while you live in it. If Christ is in the heart, the world will be in its proper place. If you are clothed with the sun, the moon will be under your feet. O what blessedness to have our conversation in heaven; to have our affections set on things above, where Christ sits at the right hand of God!

It was a custom in Rome, when the emperor went on some grand day, in all his imperial pomp and splendor, to have an officer go before him, with smoking flax, crying out, *Sic transit gloria mundi:* "So passes away the glory of the world!" This was to remind him, that all his honor and grandeur passed away, like the ascending smoke and burning flax. But, putting on Christ most effectually does this. If Christ's love be flaming within, it will burn up the love of the world in our hearts; and our affections will sit loose to all its vain pomps, and glittering vanities. We shall die to the world, before we die of it. We shall live and walk with God, and be dead to it, before we die in it.

We shall be dead to the men of this world, to their vain conversations, and sinful pleasures. We shall daily 'put off the old man with his deeds.'

Alexander the Great, when young, being asked to run in a race among the common multitude, replied, "Were I not a king's son, I should not regard my company; but being a prince, I must keep such company as is suited to my noble birth and royal dignity." What a reproof is this to many of God's children, who choose for their companions the children of the devil? But putting on Christ, you will act up to your new birth and heavenly dignity. You will not, you cannot so degrade yourself, as to choose the ungodly for your companions, their ways as your delight, nor their pastimes for your entertainment. Your soul will delight in the holy company, and heavenly conversation of the saints, who know the precious love of Christ, walk in his holy ways, and, from heartfelt experience, testify of his rich grace and glorious salvation. O how much comfort! How many spiritual blessings has my soul reaped from this! More and more are yet to come from the presence of Christ, and with the communion of saints. Blessed be Jesus, a whole eternity is to be spent in this company! We enter upon it now by faith; and the more we put on and possess Christ, the more we enjoy heaven upon earth, and taste the bliss of glory in a world of misery.

4. Putting on Christ, we shall find *growing delight in searching the scriptures*. For, says our Lord, "They testify of me" (John 5:39). The witness they bear to our Beloved is the joy of our souls. Those who are destitute of Christ, are ready to say of the scriptures, as the king of Israel said of Micaiah, "I hate them, for they do not prophesy good concerning me, but evil." But, we find that they

Happy Consequences of thus Putting On Christ

prophesy good, and nothing but good—even the good will and free love of God to us in Christ.

Do we meet with a curse in scripture? We may write under it, "This fell upon my dear Savior!" He suffered all the wrath of it; he drank up all the deadly poison in it, "he died for our sins, according to the scriptures," (1 Cor. 15:3) "He was made a curse for us" (Gal. 3:13). Says Paul, "I declare unto you the gospel, by which you are saved, if you keep in memory," or hold fast Christ and his salvation as the joyful news of the gospel. Thus, by the holy scriptures we are taught the preciousness of Christ, the greatness of his love, and the fullness of his salvation. Putting on Christ, as revealed in the scriptures, makes the scriptures precious to our believing hearts. If our hearts are at any time warmed with love, and burn with joy, it is because our Lord does, as he did to his first disciples after his resurrection, 'open the scriptures' to us, and 'open our understanding' to them. Warm hearts and burning affections, which are not caused by a solid, rational understanding of the scriptures, are to be suspected as delusion: as they spring not from Christ's truths, they promote not his glory.

Again, do we find any blessing pronounced? We may write under it, 'This is ours; it comes to us from our loving Father, through our dear Saviour.' For, "Blessed be the God and Father of our Lord Jesus Christ, who has blessed us with *all* spiritual blessings in Christ Jesus" (Eph. 1:3). There is not one blessing we can want, or that a God of infinite love can bestow, but it is ours in Christ, and we are sure to partake of it.

Do we read a sweet and precious promise? We may safely claim it as ours. Let us never draw back, or stagger at the promise through unbelief. For, having Christ, all the promises are *in him*, and all are ours in him; and all shall be fulfilled in us and to us, to the honor and glory of God by him. "For if God spared not his own Son—but delivered him up for us all—how shall he not *with him* also freely give us all things?"(Rom. 8:32)—Now look earnestly at this blessed text. Though every word is replete with love, and big with joy, yet, in transcribing it, these two words, *with him*, struck me greatly. Pray mind them. Christ is God's free gift to his people. He is given to be a covenant to them, a refuge for them, a head of influence over them, a Saviour to the uttermost of them, and the bread of life to feed and nourish them up unto eternal life. Now, have you received this precious free gift of the Father's love—his beloved Son? Have you put on Christ? Then consider, after such a wonderful gift to us, from the loving heart of a gracious God, how is it possible for him to withhold any blessing from us? God's own Son was the greatest gift God could bestow. How then, shall be not, *with him*, also, *freely* give us *all things* — *all* temporal good things— *all* spiritual blessings—eternal glory also? For *all* are secured to us in the new covenant; promised to us in the scriptures; and shall certainly be enjoyed by us, in and with Christ, for our present and eternal welfare, to the glory of God. Take then the holy scriptures, which are all given by inspiration of God, and claim them as the charter of your heavenly Father's love, and as the deeds of your rich patrimony in Christ.

5. Putting on Christ, you will *humbly submit to all God's dispensations, both in providence and grace.* For you will see the wise hand of God, and the loving heart of a Father in both. Paul exhorts, "Rejoice evermore. Pray without ceasing. In every thing give thanks." Here is spiritual joy opposed to all kinds of sorrow; prayer to every want and distress; and giving thanks to all murmur-

Happy Consequences of thus Putting On Christ

ing and complaining in times of adversity. Mind the reason, "For this is the will of God in Christ Jesus concerning you" (1 Thess. 5:16,17). Then may the Christ-clothed sinner say, 'This is the will of *my* loving Father in Christ concerning *me*. He loves *me* in Christ; he chose *me* in him; he rejoices over me in him; he ever rests in his love to me in him; and he can intend nothing but good to me in him: therefore I will constantly rejoice in my God, pray to him, and cease not to give him thanks: for I see nothing but grace in his will, wisdom in his ways, and love in his heart towards me. I cannot, I dare not reply against the sovereign will of my gracious God, or say unto my Father, what are you doing? For my Lord hath told me, and I record this soul-satisfying truth in my mind, "What I do you know not now, but you shall know hereafter" (John 13:7).'

Therefore, instead of vainly attempting to unravel the mazes of providences, to comprehend the deep mysteries of grace, and to explain all the hidden arena of the one, and to justify the methods of God in the other, I will humbly fall down and silently adore, simply believing this joyful truth; "For we know *all things* work together for good to those who love God, to those who are the called according to his purpose" (Rom. 8:28). O what cause have I to rejoice in my God, and to give thanks unto him! For, he hath called me according to his purpose; his blessed purpose is answered upon me; I have come to, do believe in, and put on his beloved Son, as the glory of my mind, the joy of my memory, and the triumph of my conscience. Now God and I are one in Christ; his will is mine; and I desire my will to be wholly conformed to, and entirely swallowed up in his.' O how sweet! thus to find our vain reasonings, and every high thing which exalts itself against the knowledge of God, cast down, and every thought brought into captivity to the obedience of Christ!

6. You will *confess Christ on earth*, and your conversation will be in heaven. Jesus Christ the same, yesterday, today, and for ever, will be the end of your conversation. For, out of the abundance of what is in your mind, memory and conscience, concerning your Beloved, your tongue will speak to his glory, and your conversation will be seasoned with the savor of his love and grace. Alas! how little spiritual, experimental discourse is now to be heard? A conversation too much prevails among professors, which is trifling, and to as little edification, as though they were to tell of the famous exploits of heroes, Tom Thumb, Robin Hood and Jack the Giant-killer.

I have often promised myself much pleasure and profit, from the company of professors, in hearing and speaking of the things of Christ; but have left them sadly grieved and disappointed. Indeed, by the appearance and conversation of some I have met with, I would not have known that they professed to know anything of our dear Savior's love, had it not been whispered in my ear, that is a member of Dr.____'s church; and that a member of Mr.____'s church. One could wish the real members of Christ to give better evidence of their being such, by their conversation.

O what a pity that that little member the tongue, which is able to set on fire the conversation, and warm the heart with love, should be dumb to our precious Immanuel's salvation and glory; while it can so glibly talk of vanities and trifles! But when Christ is put on in the mind, memory and conscience, he will be uppermost on the tongue. The heart will be pained, if the tongue is restrained from speaking of him. We shall say with David,

Happy Consequences of thus Putting On Christ

"My mouth shall show forth your righteousness, and your salvation all the day; for I know no end thereof" (Psa. 71:15). "Come and hear all you who fear God—and I will declare what he has done for my soul" (Psa. 66:16). When the heart truly believes unto righteousness, then the tongue will be a ready member to make confession of Christ and his salvation.

And to encourage us herein, our Lord says, "Whosoever shall confess me before men, him will I confess before my Father, who is in heaven" (Matt. 10:32). See how Christ will honor those who confess him! Greater honor cannot be conferred on us sinful worms of the earth, than to be confessed before the glorious Majesty of heaven, by his only begotten Son. Imagine, that you see and hear Christ thus speaking to his Father in heaven: 'O righteous Father, behold that poor sinner is not ashamed of me and my words, but boldly confesses me before men, as his only Saviour. He is a faithful witness to the truth of my word, and the power of my grace. He confesses that all his hope of pardon from thee is in my blood; all his dependence for justification in your sight, is in my righteousness; and all his expectation of being saved from sin, death and hell, is from my grace. He confesses me to be his portion. He follows me in the regeneration. He denies himself the vain pleasures, and sinful delights of a wicked world. He cannot be conformed to it, nor live unto himself and sin. O holy Father, I confess him before thee, as one of my dear brethren—the purchase of my blood, and the subject of my grace. Father, I will that he may possess that peace from thee, which I made by the blood of my cross; and enjoy your love shed abroad in his heart by the Holy Spirit *now*, and hereafter be with me, to behold my glory.'

O most glorious confession of miserable sinners, by our ever-loving Saviour, Advocate and Intercessor! The thought of it is enough to fire our hearts with love, and ever engage our tongues to confess Christ before men. But then, what inconceivable, what ineffable joy will it afford us, to hear Christ confess us before his Father, when the world shall be in flames, and the ungodly are crying to the rocks and mountains to fall on them, and to hide them from the presence of God and the wrath of the Lamb, saying, "The great day of his wrath is come, and who shall be able to stand!"

Ah, disciples of such a loving Lord, are not you as I am, ashamed for having been too often ashamed of Christ and his words before men? This *false shame* is a bold intruder. Well may we weep, to think of the advantage he has gained over us. But, by putting on Christ, as our greatest glory, we shall shake off *false shame* as our vilest enemy. When Christ is within us, *Shame* will hide his pitiful head, and skulk away from us. Possessing Christ, we shall boldly confess him. Christ enjoyed in the mind, memory and conscience, will make the Christian thrive, and rejoice in this blessed work.

Chapter 10

On the Use and Abuse
of Past Experience.

If Christ be put on, we shall not rest satisfied with past experience. Alas! how many are settled upon a shelter of their own making, saying, in the apathy of their soul, "The Lord will not do good, neither will he do evil" (Zeph. 1:12). Just as if they were to say, 'The Lord cares not for the prosperity of our souls. He regards not whether we are lively and spiritual, or slothful and carnal; whether we confess him or not. He will neither bless the one, nor chastise the other.' Such being settled upon their argument, are quite careless and secure. For they can remember, that formerly, some work passed upon their hearts. At such a time, and in such a place, they had what they call, a *Bethel visit*. They can look back, five, ten, or twenty years ago, and call to mind that they did then know something of what they call the grace of God; and they can now assert, 'once in grace, always in grace,' and vainly conclude, all is well. There is scarcely a frame of mind more to be deplored, dreaded, and deprecated than this. Lord, keep my soul ever watchful against it! Save me from falling into it!

How differently Peter speaks! "If so be that you have tasted that the Lord is gracious," — what then? sit down in sloth and ease — live upon what you formerly tasted, and be satisfied? No! — "But coming unto Jesus, as unto a living stone" (1 Pet. 2:3, 4). Here is a continued act of the soul. Christ lives to communicate fresh blessings. We are not to rest on the dead foundation of former barren notions; but constantly to exercise our faith upon him, as the living foundation of our hope; coming unto him as the life of our souls, and the source of our comforts, that we may appear as *lively stones*, for ornament and beauty in the spiritual building. Thus shall we confess and honor Christ before men, and evince that we are alive to his glory.

Though past experiences are not to be rested in, or lived upon; yet by no means should they be forgotten. We should call to mind the Lord's dealing with us, and kindness to us in days that are past. But to what end? Merely to get evidence, that formerly the Lord was gracious to us, that we may indulge present sloth? Nay, but to quicken our present coming to Christ; to animate us to fresh confidence in him; to stir us up to seek fresh comfort from him, fellowship with him, and conformity to him, that we may more boldly confess him. Observe how David reasons in regard to past experience. "The Lord, who delivered me out of the paw of the lion, and the bear, will deliver me out of the hand of this Philistine." Here is present confidence, excited by past experience. Hence see how he puts on the Lord, and arms himself afresh with the strength of his God. He says to Goliath, "I come to you in the name of the Lord of hosts." How does he honor his Lord, by the faith of his heart and the confession of his tongue? And see how the Lord honored him (1 Sam. 17).

On the Use and Abuse of Past Experience

The death of past experience, is the resurrection of present distrust and distress. Living upon past experience, is the death of present exercise of faith on Christ. Every experience of his mercy looks two ways: it satisfies present want, and is a pledge of future hope: and excites to greater confidence in the Lord. Therefore, recall your Lord's dealings with you, to encourage you to put him on afresh, for present experience of his love and power; that you may be constantly telling of his goodness, and declaring the wonders of his love.

Again, as to present dispositions and feelings.—If we put on Christ, we shall neither over-rate, nor undervalue them. An extreme on either side is hurtful. Some look more by their disposition, and live more upon their feelings, than they do upon the word of truth, and the fullness of the grace of Christ. Hence, they do not see, nor confess the glory of Christ, shining in the fundamental doctrines of the gospel: such as God's everlasting love to and choice of sinners in Christ—the sovereign efficacy of God's grace, in quickening and converting them to Christ—his fully justifying them in his righteousness—and his almighty power, in keeping them by the faith of Christ, unto eternal salvation. These glorious truths many cannot bear to hear, but say they lead to Antinomianism, and cry, "Away with all doctrines! give us warm hearts and comfortable feelings." But these doctrines lead to Christ, center on him, and nourish and build up our souls in the faith of him. And if warm hearts and comfortable feelings do not spring from the belief of these truths, and are not supported by the word of God's grace, they are not the solid, scriptural joys of the Holy Spirit; but. the effects of a warm fancy, and a heated imagination. They spring from self-righteousness and self-complacency. They begin in nature, will end in nature, and deceive the soul.

This is evident, when a warm disposition and comfortable feelings are set up to establish self-confidence, and to count as nought God's displays of his everlasting love, covenant grace, and abounding mercy to sinners in Christ, revealed in his word. The Lord saith to such, "Behold, all you who kindle a fire, who compass yourselves about with sparks: walk in the light of your fire, and in the sparks that you have kindled: This you shall have at my hand, says the Lord, you shall lie down in sorrow" (Isa. 1. 11). For, we know how soon a spark goes out, and nature's fire dies away.

Do we not see this verified in professors daily? For, instead of putting on Christ, and clothing their minds with his precious truths, and living upon the glorious declarations of God's rich grace, the immutability of his counsel and covenant, ratified by the blood of Christ, and confirmed by the sacred oath of God, that the heirs of promise might have strong consolation, alas! They quit the faith of all this, to live upon what they find and feel in themselves. And hence, when their warm ideals vary, and their comfortable feelings decline, their consolation is fled and gone, like the morning mist before the meridian sun, and they sink into distress of soul, and lie down in sorrow of heart. Hence, how many professors have fallen away, gone back to seek happiness in the world, and rejected Christ's truths and ways, as gloomy and distressing?

Our Lord describes such as stony ground hearers, who receive the word with joy. It works upon their passions and affections. Just like *Pliable* in the Pilgrim's Progress: "O, says he, the hearing of these comfortable things is enough to ravish one's heart! Well, my good companion, come on. Let us mend our pace." But, says

On the Use and Abuse of Past Experience

our Lord, "They have no root in themselves," no settled understanding, no solid judgment in the revealed truths of God. "They believe for a while." Their faith is founded upon the heat of their passions, and supported by animal joys, instead of being rooted in the word of God. Hence, "in the time of temptation or trial, they fall away." So did *Pliable* at the Slough of Despond. The very first trial he met with, cooled his passions, killed his faith, and sent him back to the city of Destruction. Such not being rooted in, nor living upon "Thus saith the Lord:" not believing in their hearts the written word, nor feeding in their hearts on Christ the essential word, it is no marvel, that their flashy joys and fleshly comforts forsake them, and their confession of Christ is soon at an end. O see to it then, that you honor God's word, by the steady belief of your heart; his faithfulness and trust, by the firm reliance of your soul: so will you steadfastly cleave to Christ; and let your dispositions and feelings be what they may, still you will see and confess, Christ to be all in all to you.

Our dispositions and feelings are a very deceitful mirror to view the love of God in, or to judge of the love of God by. But in the clear glass of God's word, we behold the amazing love of his heart, in giving his beloved Son to redeem, justify and save us—the sweet declarations of his covenant love, rich grace, and precious promises to us in Christ, which are ever to accompany and comfort us. These are the only firm basis for our faith to fix on, for solid peace, spiritual joy, and abounding consolation. And if our warm dispositions and comfortable feelings do not spring from faith in these, and are not supported by and correspondent with these, we may well suspect them: for instead of putting on Christ, and glorying in him, we shall be clothed with the fool's garment of self-righteousness, and self-complacency. And instead of confessing Christ to be all in all to us, we shall swell with a high notion of our own importance and perfection; fancying ourselves to be something, when we are nothing, and go on deceiving ourselves.

But on the other hand, while some err about dispositions and feelings, placing an undue confidence in them, and over-rating them, above and beyond divine truths; others lightly esteem and undervalue them, saying, "We don't mind our dispositions and feelings: we are not to live upon them." True: we are not, be they ever so warm, lively and comfortable. But, blessed be our Lord, we are not to live without them. Warm, lively, comfortable dispositions, which spring from faith in the word of God's free grace to us in Christ, should be highly prized, and most earnestly coveted. Verily, you must be sunk into a very carnal and dead disposition indeed, and have taken up with an Antinomian faith, if you can rest satisfied without feeling spiritual warmth, liveliness and comfort, from union to, and communion with Christ our Lord and head. A spiritual man can no more live without spiritual feelings, than a natural man can without natural feelings. The spiritually quickened soul, is either feeling the sense, and groaning under the burden of the misery and wretchedness of his fallen nature, and crying to the Saviour for deliverance; or, he feels himself happy in Christ, and rejoicing in his love and salvation. For,

> *If sweet be our frame, we bless his dear name:*
> *If bitter, we pray,*
> *And Jesus so loves us, he takes it away.*

But, soul, can you go on from day to day, easy and unconcerned, without feeling the peace of God in your conscience, the love of God shed abroad in your heart, and spiritual joy in the Holy Spirit, arising from fellowship with God the Father, and his Son Jesus Christ? Can you be contented without praying, wrestling, and striving with the Lord for the enjoyment of these spiritual blessings? Truly, if you are not dead in trespasses and sins, yet be assured you are not living upon Christ: but have made a vile exchange of him, for some cursed idol. And you dare not, you cannot, say, in faith and truth, that you are confessing Christ, in heart, mouth and life, as your chief glory. The reason is plain—if the soul is destitute of spiritual affection to Christ, it can enjoy no warm inclinations, no delightful sensations, no sweet incomings of light, life, love, joy and peace from him.

But say some, "the churches are fallen asleep." More shame for them! What then? Shall we be afraid of boldly confessing Christ, lest we should disturb their repose? or because we cannot awaken them, shall we lie down, and go to sleep with them? True, Satan has rocked many professors fast asleep, in the golden cradle of worldly ease and prosperity; yet, my dear brethren in Christ, we have a life-giving, soul-quickening Head. Surely, we can never think of him, as Elijah mockingly told the priests of Baal, "Perhaps he is a god who sleeps:" and though we cry to him, yet he will not hear us, quicken, nor comfort us. Away with such sleepy, unbelieving, dishonoring thoughts of Christ!—He delights in the prosperity of his people. He is a living Head of influence to them. He is a quickening Spirit in them. His ears are ever open to their prayers. He bids them to come unto him for life. And his watch-word to all the children of the light and of the day is "Do not sleep as others do" (1 Thess. 5:6).

Let us then watch against a sleepy disposition, and beware of sleeping professors, lest we get into, and rest satisfied with a notion of union to Christ, without putting him on in the life and power of faith in our hearts, and feeling the comforts of communion with him, and the blessings of light, life, holiness, peace and joy from, him. Avoid those who lightly esteem spiritual inclinations and heart-felt experience of the grace of Christ. An acquaintance of mine, who had long sat under the ministry of the greatest Antinomian of this day, observed to me of his preaching, that he painted an exceeding good Sun; but there was neither light nor heat in it, nor any communications from it. Meaning that he gave a fine description of Christ, and talked of union to him; but without expecting or receiving any sanctifying communications from him, to conform the soul to him, and cause us to bring forth the fruits of righteousness in our lives, to the honor and glory of him — such preachers, and preaching may do very well for those who never had, or have lost conviction of sin, the sense of the importance of spiritual and eternal things; and are asleep in carnal security. But, souls who are alive to God, hungering and thirsting after Christ, can no more be satisfied with such, than a hungry man can be with painted food. For, from sweet and blessed experience, we know and confess, that Christ fills the hungry with good things: that in waiting upon him, we renew our strength: that in coming to him, he gives us rest, and refreshes our souls. For he is not a fountain sealed, but open and communicative of the streams of his love, which make glad our hearts. We feel that he is the Sun of righteousness, who arises upon our souls with healing grace, and pardoning love under his wings. He sheds his warm rays, enlightening beams, and enlivening influence upon us, whereby we grow in grace, and in the knowledge of him, delight to walk in fellowship with him, and love to devote our bodies, souls and spirits daily to his glory. Hence it is, that we glory of him, rejoice in him, and boldly confess him to be the chiefest among ten thousand to our hearts, as our Saviour from all sin; and altogether lovely in our sight, to sanctify us throughout in body, soul and spirit.

O Christians! That is a most blessed disposition of soul, and a most glorious confession which Paul mentions, "Now, thanks be unto God, who *always* causes us to triumph in Christ, and makes manifest the savor of his knowledge by us in every place" (2 Cor. 2:14). You can never, never too much triumph of Christ, and in him. Though in ourselves we are perfect weakness, and sinfulness, and have neither joy nor victory; yet in Christ we should ever be shouting the triumph of his victory; for over every enemy that is against us, "*we are more than conquerors*, through him who loved us" (Rom. 8:37). So confess Christ, as to make every place resound with shouts of his victorious grace.

But is it ever whispered in your ear? "You make too much of Christ, confess too much of him: and rob God the Father of his glory." It is often in mine. But we may be fully assured, that this comes from the spirit of Antichrist. For, Paul declares with thanks, that it is God who causes us *always* to triumph in Christ, etc. Is it so? Is it the peculiar work of God to cause us to confess Christ, to triumph in him, and to make manifest the savor of his knowledge? Why then, saith the Antinomian spirit of sloth and licentiousness, 'let us be still and quiet; there is no need of any activity, labor and diligence of ours.' But, saith the Spirit of Christ to his members, 'stir up the gift of God that is in you.' Be not slothful. Pray, wrestle and strive with God, for that power which he giveth to them who have no might. Give the Lord no rest, constantly cry to him to strengthen you by his Spirit in the inner man, that you may be ready and obedient to every good word and work for your Lord's glory. Is it God who works in us both to will and to do of his good pleasure? This is a reason, why we should work out our own salvation—be diligent and active in the use of those means of grace, which are connected with, and are productive of, the comfortable hope of salvation and glory. Do we expect the Lord to give us peace always, by all means? Then let us be always diligent in attending on all those means, in which he will be found by us, and bestow peace upon us: so shall we always triumph in Christ; and it will be our greatest glory to confess him, and glory of him. "Therefore, my beloved brethren, be steadfast, immovable, always abounding in the work of the Lord, for as much as you know, that your labor is not in vain in the Lord" (1 Cor. 15:58).

Putting on we will be daily looking to, and joyfully longing for, the coming of your Lord. Christ cannot dwell in us by faith—but we shall find our hearts longing to be with him in glory. A taste of his wonderful love on earth, begets desires to enjoy its fullness in heaven. What precious words of my Lord are these! O my soul, clothe yourself more and more with them. "Father, I *will* that those you have given me to be with me where I am, and to see my glory" (John 17:24). "I will come again to receive you to myself, that where I am, there you may be also" (John 14:3). My fellow Christians, what are we about! Why are our heads at any time hanging down, and our hearts dejected? Why rather, are not our hearts all on fire at these words, and our souls ardently longing for our Lord's coming again to receive us to himself, that we may be eternally with him, and forever behold his glory? Truly, it will be so, if Christ be put on, if our mem-

On the Use and Abuse of Past Experience

ories are clothed with these his precious words, and our conscience finds peace in him.

But what kills our present comforts? What deadens our joyful hope? What prevents our ardent longings after glory, immortality, and eternal life with Christ? Nothing but giving way to cursed unbelief, which gives the lie to the God of truth, and calls in question the sweet declarations and precious promises of the God of love. O beware those who water and cultivate this degenerate plant, by teaching that Christ-dishonoring, soul-dejecting doctrine, that any of Christ's sheep may so fall from grace, and perish in their sins, never to be with him to behold his glory. For this will prove like a dagger to the heart of your hope, and effectually kill your longing for the coming of your Lord. But, if Christ is put on, and his truths dwell in your memory, you will honor his words, cast away such base suggestions against his love, and joyfully sing,

> *The love divine that made me yours,*
> *Shall keep me yours forever!*

And indeed, unless the mind is clothed with, the memory retains, and the conscience is living upon the word of Christ's grace, the declarations of his love, the promises of his lips, and the unchangeable purposes of his heart, instead of longing for his coming, we shall tremble at the thought of his appearing. But to prevent this, our Lord, well knowing how foolish we are, and how slow of heart to believe, says, "I give to my sheep eternal life, they shall never perish; neither shall any pluck them out of my hand" (John 10:25). Words big with comfort, and replete with joy! Enough to silence forever the gainsayings, and put to perpetual shame, all who give our Lord the lie, by asserting that any of his sheep may perish. Yea, sufficient to make accursed unbelief skulk away, and hide its baneful head.

Now, if you put on Christ's truth, you will love his appearing. But if you receive the devil's lie that there is a possibility that you, a believer in Christ, may not enjoy eternal life, but may be plucked out of Christ's hand, and perish everlastingly; then you will dread the very thought of Christ's coming. Instead of obeying your Lord, when he bids you lift up your head with joy, for your redemption draws near, you will hang down your head with sorrow, dreading lest your damnation draws near.

To encourage our longing for his coming, our Lord assures us, "Because I live, you shall live also" (John 14:9). "No," says the father of lies, "though you may live a life of faith upon the Son of God for a season—yet you may fall short of eternal life and glory in the end." But that is impossible, unless Christ himself is dead. A godly widow in great distress, with her children crying for bread; said, "Children be comforted, for God lives." Some time after, one of the children seeing its mother weep, said to her, 'Is God dead now?' So, we may ask those who talk of saints falling from grace, so as to perish in hell, "Is Christ their Savior dead?" No, he lives! "He ever lives to make intercession for, and to save to the *uttermost*, ALL who come to God by him!" (Heb. 7:25). Therefore, "When Christ who is our life shall appear, then shall we also appear with him in glory" (Col. 3:4). Having put on Christ, we shall uphold his inspired truths, to refute all conspired lies against his glory and our comfort. Thus shall we keep up our longings to be with him. Have we seen by the eye of faith, the ignominy, agonies, sorrows and sufferings, which Christ endured in the days of his flesh, for our sins, and for our salvation? Have we tasted and felt in the power of faith, the blessings and comforts of his humbling grace, dying love and risen power? Have we put on Christ as the glory of our mind, the joy of our memory, and the comfort of our conscience? Do we not long and desire to see that blessed head which was crowned with thorns for our sakes, crowned with glory and honor; and to be forever with that dear *man* in glory, who so dearly obtained eternal life and glory for us? Surely we must, "knowing in ourselves, that we have in heaven a far better, and an enduring substance" (Heb. 10:34). For, all on this side death is shadow: all beyond it is substance.

"Knowing in ourselves," O it is this joyful knowledge, which sharpens the edge of our desire, and quickens our longing to be with Christ. And by putting on Christ, we have this blessed knowledge in ourselves, and assuredly know, that we are heirs of God, and joint-heirs with Christ, and shall certainly enjoy the heavenly inheritance with him. "Ah, but," says an enlightened soul, "I cannot long for Christ's coming, because I see myself so vile, so full of sin, so prone to every evil, so backward to every good—so what title can I have to the kingdom of Christ?" As to your title, in and from yourself, you have as good a one, as any saint; yes, or any of the apostles, Paul, Peter, or John ever had—which is none at all. Yet, this did not prevent their longing, nor should it your longing for the coming of Christ; for he forbids our fears, and encourages our joy, with, "Fear not little flock, it is your Father's good pleasure to *give* you the kingdom!" (Luke 12:32). So that you see our title to glory comes to us, by the promise of the free grace, free love, and gift of our Father's good pleasure. Faith claims our title to it, interest in it, and fitness for it in Jesus, his beloved Son.

"For to all who did receive Him, He gave them the right to be children of God, to those who believe in His name" (John 1:12). If you truly believe in Jesus, you are a son of God, an heir of God, and a joint-heir with Christ. So that putting on Christ, we know in ourselves that we have in heaven an enduring substance. As to your feeling your vileness and sorrowing for your sinfulness, it is clear evidence of your fitness for, and of your being a blessed heir of Christ's kingdom. For says he, "Blessed are the poor in Spirit; for theirs is the kingdom of heaven" (Matt. 5:3). The deeper sense of our vileness, the more poverty of spirit—the more blessedness. Why so? Because hereby the soul is cut off from self-righteous pride, self-confidence, and self-glorying; and the Savior gets all the glory from the poor humble sinner's heart. He learns more and more to put on Christ, to trust him more, and to glory only in him, as in God; seeing himself "in Christ Jesus, who is made unto him wisdom, righteousness, sanctification and redemption; that according as it is written, he who glories, let him *glory in the Lord*" (1 Cor. 1:30, 31). O it is blessed work indeed, when the soul is brought to this. Hence it is that the soul looks and longs "for the Savior, the Lord Jesus Christ, who shall change our vile body, that it may be fashioned like unto his glorious body" (Phil. 3:21).

These feelings of our vileness and sinfulness, are what every saint in Christ experiences. Paul, and his brethren in Christ, found just same. Hear him crying "O wretched man that I am, who shall deliver me from the body of this death!" (Rom. 7:24). Yet he declares, "We are the true circumcision." Our hearts are cut off from our old, legal, self-righteous dependences for justification. "We have no confidence in the flesh." We have nothing in ourselves whereof to glory. Yet, "we rejoice in Christ Jesus" (Phil. 3:3). Rejoice, that we are in him, and that "no condemnation" is against us (Rom. 8). Rejoice "that we are complete in him" (Col 2:10). We rejoice that "we are accepted in him" (Eph. 1:6). We rejoice that we are presented in him, without spot of sin unto salvation (Eph. 1:27). And rejoice, that when he shall appear, then shall we appear with him in glory (Col 3:4). For though we see nothing in ourselves, to afford us the least spark of joy, yet in Christ we have an inexhaustible spring of joy — a never-failing storehouse of joy. Hence we are called upon to "Rejoice *in the Lord always*; and again I say rejoice" (Phil. 4:4).

This joy is the joy of the Holy Spirit. That joy, which the scriptures warrant and excite to; springs from faith in Jesus; and by putting on Christ, this spiritual joy in him, and longing for his coming, will be kept up, under all the sense and feeling of our own vileness. For, while in this tabernacle, we shall groan, being burdened (2 Cor. 5:4). This ever was, now is, and will be the lot of all saints. But, what do they groan under? What are they burdened with? A body of sin and death. That you groan under this, is a joyful proof that you are a saint; that you have a new nature, and are a new creature in Christ. For, the dead in sin feel not this burden. They groan not under it. They cry not for deliverance from it. "But we, who have the first-fruits of the Spirit, groan within ourselves" (Rom. 8:23). "O wretched man that I am!" says Paul. It is our new and holy nature, that feels the weight, and groans under the burden of our old body of sin and death—"Who shall deliver us from this?" Thanks be to God, who giveth us the victory, through Jesus Christ. By faith we receive it. And there is no relief for us but by believing in, looking to, and living upon this sin-atoning

Lamb of God, who was crucified for our sins. Soon, at his glorious appearing we shall be forever delivered.

Hear then the conclusion of the whole matter—the sum of all I have been writing. This is my grand aim in this work, to quicken your soul and mine, to live and walk in constant communion, and holy fellowship, with God the Father, and his Son Jesus Christ, through the power of the Holy Spirit. O may the Lord bless and make it subservient to this purpose, that while our souls enjoy the comfort of this, his blessed name may have all the honor and glory, from our hearts, lips and lives. O you believing, Christ-clothed sinners, well may you say, 'Fly swiftly, you moments, till Jesus returns.' Well may you be looking and longing for Christ's coming, to take you from all the sins, groans, pains and sorrows, which ye are the subjects of, while present in the body, and absent from the Lord. For, O what ineffable joy, and boundless glory, shall we enter, when 'absent from the body, and present with the Lord!'

Come, take a fresh view of it now. Let faith realize the prospect. Let hope enter into that which is within the veil. View it as at hand, and yourself just entering into it. See your Lord in full possession of it for you. For Jesus our forerunner, is for us entered (Heb. 6:20). O that in the view of faith, in the joy of hope, and in the triumph of the love of Christ, we may be constantly crying, 'Make haste, my beloved;' 'come, Lord Jesus, come quickly.' Even so. Amen.

Other Books from C.C.R. Publishing:

That Christ May Have Preeminence
Various Authors:
Isaac Ambrose, Samuel Davies, Thomas Watson, Octavius Winslow, Jonathan Edwards, Richard Sibbes, John Flavel and Thomas Chalmers
242 pages | ISBN: 978-1484998465

The School of Calvary & The Passion For Souls
Author: John Henry Jowett
142 pages | ISBN: 978-1494878931

The Anxious Inquirer After Salvation
Author: John Angell James, 1834
144 pages | ISBN: 978-1-4960-1437-5

William Mason lived from 1719 – 29 September 1791, and is best remembered for his book of daily meditations, *A Spiritual Treasury for the Children of God*, and for his explanatory and experimental notes to Pilgrim's Progress.

Written in 1773, *The Believer's Pocket Companion,* has such redeeming direction and assuring comfort for the Christian life and walk.

Made in the USA
Charleston, SC
07 August 2015